MW01147152

How to Shepherd Children in a World Full of Wolves

through a caring, nurturing children's ministry

Herb Owen

Church Growth Institute
Providing Practical Tools for Growth
P.O. Box 4404, Lynchburg, VA 24502

Editor: Cindy G. Spear
Designer: Carolyn R. Phelps
Editorial and Design Assistant: Tamara Johnson

Scriptures in this text are the King James and New
Century Versions of the Holy Bible.
New Century Version ©, 1987, 1988, 1991 by Word
Publishing, Dallas, TX 75039. Used by permission.

CONTENTS

Preface 7

Chapter One 13
Why Is Working with Kids So Important?
How Can We Do It God's Way?

Chapter Two 35
Can God Really Use Me?

Chapter Three 47
Goals for Your Ministry

Chapter Four 61
How Can I Reach New Children?

Chapter Five 71
Visiting in the Homes of Children

Chapter Six 85
Teaching the Bible to Children

Chapter Seven 115
Leading a Child to Christ

Chapter Eight 129
Seeing the Potential

Bibliography 143

Publishers of Curriculum, Children's Programs,
Teaching Resources, and Teacher Training Materials... 153

Scriptures Relating to Our Ministry to Children 155

PREFACE

PREFACE

*"Come, ye children, hearken unto me:
I will teach you the fear of the Lord"* (Ps. 34:11).

One day when I was a child it occurred to my parents that if their son were going to grow to become a "good little boy," they needed to get the little guy in church. So off we went.

We soon found ourselves active members in a busy denominational church. My dad became a deacon, Mom was a soloist in the choir, and I became the "official church kid." I was the little guy who played the leading role in the Christmas play, and I was the kid who followed the custodian around the church after the Lord's supper, drinking all of the unused grape juice! We were very active, always attending church at least twice a week.

I remember another little boy at that church. Although I can't recall his name, I do know he was a thief. I remember it well because one Sunday morning, during the general assembly in the Junior Department, he took my toy truck and pocketed it as his own. I reported the incident to the proper authorities who, after a quick investigation, decided the truck was mine. Their decision was right, of course; but the way they arrived at it was a little questionable. Since I was a "good little boy" they reasoned I wouldn't lie. So I kept the truck.

But there was another result with more serious implications. I never remember seeing that little boy back in the Junior Department again.

I was the good kid; he was the thief. A big difference? No, not really. We both shared a common problem. Neither of us knew Christ as Savior!

The church soon moved to the suburbs into a new

and grander building. But something happened in our lives. We didn't enjoy getting up on Sunday mornings anymore. The youth meetings were boring (they really were), and my mom and dad didn't feel the same commitment they had felt before. There was a good reason for their feelings. You see, they didn't know Christ either!

Although I was "raised in church" as a child, it wasn't until I was a junior in high school and met a Christian friend that the truth of the Gospel began to grow clear. And finally, near the end of the eleventh grade, I trusted Christ as my Savior at the little church where my friend and his family were members.

The church building was small...only 168 folding chairs...half light wood and half dark. (They had bought them from the funeral home at two different times as the parlor "upgraded" to something better.) There was no organ. (I didn't know you could even call it a church if it didn't have an organ!) The pianist was age 13, and she knew only two offertories. There was no church bulletin. Compared to the church I had attended a few years ago, this was a shoddy little organization.

But Christ was there. And many people were there who soon cared about me. They were willing to invite me back to play my clarinet in the revival service each night until finally it all sank in and I trusted Christ as Savior.

There are kids at your church like I was back then. They are there each Sunday, but they don't quite get it all. Their moms and dads will be sure they are faithfully present at the services until finally they begin to grow up a little and decide that all of this isn't really for them. Then you'll see them only now and then. After a while, they won't be there at all.

You also have kids like that little guy who stole my truck. I always wondered who he was. He was probably from a weak home (or from a broken one), and taking what he wanted was the only way he knew. Every now and then I wonder what happened to him. You and I could probably guess.

A lot more kids never even enter a church – cute little guys and girls who will grow up and follow whatever expressions of ungodliness are popular in their neighborhoods. And lives that were meant to glorify God will likely end in failure.

It all sounds discouraging until we remember that God is in the business of fixing broken lives and intercepting kids on the way down before they hit bottom. That's where you and I come into the picture.

Since the day I trusted Christ, God has allowed me to become involved in the lives of thousands of kids. Others are out there waiting for you to come along and love them and teach them to love the Lord! So read this book with an open mind. And the next time you drive to the store, look at the boys and girls on their bikes and in the playgrounds. Do they know Christ? Are they from Christian homes? Could God use you to influence them for eternity?

God can use us in amazing ways to help boys and girls turn to Christ. We can teach them to love the Lord. We can teach them to pray. We can show them how to obey. We can help them live the lives God intended when He created them.

God's plan is for every Christian to be busy, using the gifts given by the Lord himself, to minister to other believers and reach out into a lonely world of people who need the Lord.

What we want to accomplish in this book

This little book will help you think about what you can do, and provide some specific suggestions you can use right away. On these pages, we will:

- Discover the importance of ministering to children.

- Learn together what our ultimate objectives are and discover the tools God has provided to help us accomplish them.

- Help you determine if you are a person God can use to reach boys and girls.

- List the goals of a successful children's ministry.

- Give you ideas to help you reach the boys and girls of your town for Christ.

- Teach you how to visit the homes of children.

- Share some tested ideas to make you a better Bible teacher.

- Offer you tips to help in leading a child to Christ.

- Visualize your present potential for ministry.

- Provide a list of Scripture references that will help in your ministry to children.

- Acquaint you with resources that will help you in your ministry.

God has provided each one of His people with spiritual gifts to equip them to do His work. That's because He has place for all of us. And He has a place for you!

Chapter One

WHY IS WORKING WITH KIDS SO IMPORTANT? HOW CAN WE DO IT GOD'S WAY?

Chapter One

WHY IS WORKING WITH KIDS SO IMPORTANT? HOW CAN WE DO IT GOD'S WAY?

I was youth and children's pastor at the church. Excitement mounted as plans for the new building began to take shape. There were lots of meetings, of course. One of these gatherings dealt with the question of what, exactly, we felt we needed in this new building. As the youngest person in the room, I sat quietly in a corner and watched the men at work. The auditorium would need to seat so many, and the platform should look like this, and we needed a lot of classrooms. The parking lots would go here, and the sanctuary would be designed like a church the men had seen in another city. And on it went.

As the self-appointed advocate of the kids in the church, I had a few ideas of my own. And soon I worked up enough nerve to bring a few before the throne.

The response was firm and quickly executed. The kids weren't paying for this, I was told. We can just make do with what was made available. These men meant well, but it soon became apparent that my priorities were not important to them at all.

Perhaps the attitude of your church isn't that bad. But when we begin to talk about investing time and money in children, questions quickly arise. People want to know where all that money is going. Do we really need those buses and vans? Something has to go from the budget. We can't take it out of missions, of course. And insurance rates are going up. Why can't we cut the children's programs in half?

Are children's ministries really important?

Why are our ministries to boys and girls important? Aren't we just baby-sitting? Does it really help to bring children in from unchurched homes? Don't they face the same problems when they leave? And shouldn't the members' children be in the auditorium with the big folks, learning to sit up straight in church?

On a more personal level, why should *you* get involved? Isn't this work best left to the professionals? Or shouldn't younger (or older and more mature) people do this? Are there not others with more experience who could do it better? Can anything really important be accomplished by your involvement?

What it's like being a kid in America

Think a minute about the kids of our nation. Or better yet, consider the boys and girls in your town. What are they like? What is going on in their lives? What problems do they face? The statistics are not lovely at all.

1. One-fourth of all children live with only one parent.

2. Over two million cases of child neglect and abuse are reported annually.

3. Over a million children are born to unmarried women each year. That's over 25% of all children born in the U.S.!

4. Over a million kids under 18 are arrested each year. That includes:

    *   Over 2,000 for murder
    *   Just under 5,000 for rape
    *   Almost 50,000 for assault
    *   Close to 100,000 for vandalism
    *   And over 60,000 runaways are caught yearly

5. Over 2,000 juveniles are in jail on any given day.

6. Almost a million unmarried couple households include children under age 15.

7. Most teens now consider sexual involvement as part of the normal dating process.

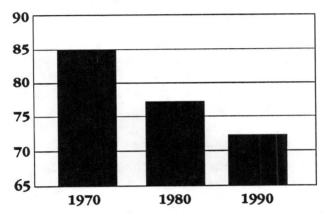

What percent of the children in America live with both parents?

The chart and figures above do not include the millions of boys and girls who escape the problems normally thought more serious, yet become failures as adults. They will become the shattered pieces of broken homes, the fathers who put work before family, and the countless millions in America who live as if there were no God at all.

3 Basic Truths

It's not hard to realize that there is a job to be done. The young people of our nation are in a mess. Families are failing and the church must do something to help. If we don't reach children with the Gospel their lives will suffer. Three basic truths make that statement ring even more true.

---

1. **We were created to glorify God.**
2. **Only when we fulfill our destiny can we enjoy life to the fullest.**
3. **A life lived in any other way is a failure.**

We must internalize these truths ourselves. They will totally change the way we look at people, lead to new priorities in our lives, and revolutionize how we view our ministry to children. God can use us to help kids grow to glorify God.

What is our ultimate objective?

Every soldier gets his marching orders from headquarters, so what are ours? Sure, we want to get kids in church. We want to see boys and girls trust Christ as Savior. We want to see kids say "No!" to sin. But there is more. The apostle Paul clearly laid out the ultimate objective to follow when ministering to boys and girls. It is contained in two specific truths found in Romans 8:28 and 29:

1. Everything we do must work together to accomplish one goal. "And we know that all things work together for good to them that love God, to them who are called according to his purpose."

2. Our goal is to help boys and girls become like Jesus Christ. "For whom he did foreknow, he also did predestinate to be conformed to the image of his Son."

That is what Christian education is all about. Write down the following definition and keep it in your Bible.

Christian education is everything I do that helps people become like Jesus Christ.

Why do we have Sunday School? Why children's church? What about sports leagues in the church? Why do we need summer camp and children's choirs? The answers are all the same. We do the things we do to help boys and girls become like Christ.

Once I visited a church where the children's director asked me to sit in on a Sunday School class. He wanted my opinion about how things were going, so I agreed to take my family and spend the hour with the group. It all began as many other classes would begin. When I arrived I found 20 scrubbed down juniors, hair slicked back and combed and with ribbons on the girls. But it was downhill from there.

Visitors trickled in throughout the hour. Each was handed a visitor's card and pencil and spent most of the remainder of the hour trying to fill it in, often with the help of a nearby child. One boy (obviously the lowest kid in the pecking order) sheepishly entered early in the lesson to the groans of the other guys in the class. As the rest of the guys gave him grief, the teacher kept on teaching, totally ignoring what was going on. The confusion grew worse as the Sunday School superintendent entered the class several times during the lesson. There were many exciting things going on in that little room, but teaching and learning were not among them. What went wrong? Why did the teacher in charge let all this happen?

All of the activities of the church have a common goal: we are here to help people become like Christ. Evaluate everything you are doing to see if your activity is helping you get there. Ask yourself the pivotal question: will what I am about to do help the kids become like the Lord? Looking at your ministry from this perspective will quickly bring things in line and help you know if you are on your way to success.

How can we know if we are successful?

Success and failure in the business world are easy to discover. All businesses have one main objective: it is called "return on investment." Money is invested in the business. The idea is to get back what you put in and a whole lot more. If business does not go as planned, strange things soon begin to happen. One day the word gets out that you have fallen behind in your bills, and suppliers stop shipping the things you need. Soon there's not enough money to meet payroll. And eventually the lights won't come on because you didn't pay the bill. That's okay, because nobody is around to need them anyway! If a business does not bring in a return on the investment of the owners, the business is soon abandoned.

Church work is not that simple, however. There are several good reasons why it is more difficult for us to identify success. "Growing in Christ" is hard to measure. You can count bodies present on Sunday morning and record the number of verses memorized. But these figures alone do not reflect Christian growth.

A young children's pastor told me of his frustration in preparing for camp. He did his best to get everything ready. The needed church funds were finally approved. But suddenly there were emergency meetings in the church treasurer's office. Money was tight. For a day or so there was discussion as to whether there should be camp at all. Finally, the camp won out and the checks were printed. But after they decided that it was too late to cancel the camp, the pastor warned, "I hope we get some baptisms out of this; that's all I can say."

Surely winning the lost was a goal of that camp, and fifteen, in fact, trusted Christ. Six of those children followed the Lord in baptism the following Sunday night. But salvation decisions and baptisms alone aren't enough to judge the success and failure of our ministries.

Another problem in measuring our success is that sometimes the process of transforming an unsaved child into a loving Christian takes many years. Scripture frequently reminds us that discipleship is a lifelong process. In fact, Jesus Himself reminds us that "...the harvest is the end of the world" (Matt. 13:39).

It is easy to busy ourselves with activity that does not accomplish a thing! The kids in that Sunday School class I visited would have better spent the morning watching a Christian video. Wherever we find ourselves in the Lord's service, we must remember why we are there.

The dimensions of Christian growth

In what ways do children become like Christ? Surely Christian growth is more than being good and doing right.

The answer is again found in the Bible. When Luke tells us about the early days of Jesus Christ on this earth, he provides four specific guidelines for helping children grow in Christ.

"And Jesus increased in wisdom and stature,
and in favour with God and man" (Luke 2:52).

Look carefully at this verse. In it we find a master plan to help us plan our ministries. If we want our children to become like Christ, we must help them grow as He did. Christian growth is four-dimensional and impacts every part of our lives.

We must help children grow:
• *Mentally* in wisdom.
• *Physically* in stature.
• *Spiritually* in favor with God.
• *Socially* in favor with man.

So what does it all mean? How can I make my ministry to children four-dimensional?

Helping children grow in wisdom

The book of Proverbs is truly a textbook on the subject of wisdom. Several years ago I spent many morning devotional times translating the book to a level a child could understand. Early in the book I discovered nine reasons why God wants us to study the book. You could call these:

Solomon's 9 Goals of Wisdom
Proverbs 1:2-4

---

1. That you might become good at using the truths you have learned.

2. That you would become a disciplined person.

3. That you would understand what is right and wrong.

4. That you would learn from your mistakes and from the mistakes of others.

5. That you would choose right.

6. That you would learn the difference between truth and error.

7. That you would develop strong character.

8. That you would be protected while growing in wisdom.

9. That you would learn to think carefully about what you do.

Analyze this list carefully. It contains your first set of goals for working with children. Remember this: our ultimate objective is to help kids grow to become like Christ. Our list of four dimensions tells us in what ways we should help children grow and gives us a place to start. We have *Solomon's 9 Goals of Wisdom* to help kids grow in wisdom. Keep these goals in mind when you're planning your Sunday School lesson. And keep this list on your clipboard while you're coaching the team.

The greatest mark of Christian growth is the development of godly wisdom that comes from a heart and mind filled with the things of the Lord.

What it means to grow in stature

This means more than "building strong bodies 12 ways." Our bodies are called "the dwelling place of the Holy Spirit." We most often serve God with our bodies. We can teach children to use their voices to praise and their hands to do His work. And we can teach them to be bold in sharing their faith in Christ.

Satan uses temptations to the body to destroy the spirit. When we protect kids from physical temptations, we help make it possible for them to live fruitful lives for God.

We also can provide opportunities for physical activity as part of the church program. I don't know what happens at your church, but I do know what happens at mine. During the winter kids come to the church with a Bible under one arm and a basketball under the other. The Bible is for during the service, the ball is for before and after.

So why not provide a basketball league in the church gym? All that undeveloped church property behind the auditorium would make a great baseball field. And a soccer program needs but a few simple goals, a ball, and a rulebook. (Shin guards might help a little, too!)

Several years ago a boy in our church came one Saturday morning to register for the 4th-, 5th- and 6th-grade basketball league, and he brought along his 5th-grade friend. The new boy, an obvious athlete, spent the first half of the morning in the bleachers, simply watching his buddy go through his paces.

After introducing myself and making him feel welcome, I learned that Chris was already signed up for another league. But why not be in ours, too? I told him it would be no problem with me that he played in two leagues. So I gave him an application and my sales pitch, then sent him home to talk it over with Mom and Dad.

Next Saturday morning the new boy was back, and Mom and Dad came too! I gave them the tour of the church, and tried to let them know we were nice people. They weren't too excited about church, but they thought the basketball program would be just fine! So they signed the boy up, and the whole family went home happy. However, I had a plan.

Could we use basketball to win the boy to Christ? I called the friend who had brought him, talked it over and gave him some encouragement. I probably would not be able to talk his family into letting Chris come to Sunday School. But if he should happen to spend Saturday night with his friend, surely he could come along with his buddy!

Before long it happened. The new boy showed up one Sunday evening. And he was back the next week too! Before you know it, he was coming on Sunday morning, too!

He still did not know the Lord. I knew we needed to get him away from home and surround him with Christian kids. I needed some time. So we arranged for him to go along on our annual missions trip to Mexico. And one night, outside of a simple little village church, something wonderful happened. David, the boy who had brought a visitor to basketball, led his friend to Christ!

Growing in favor with God

This is the part everyone understands best. Every church has Sunday School. We count Bibles, memorized verses, and completed lessons. We keep a record of how many are saved, how are baptized, and how many walk the aisle.

But growing spiritually is more than that. We want to create a program of discipleship to help kids grow in Christ.

*My program
is everything I do that helps me
accomplish my goals.*

We normally think of a program as something planned at a regular time. And most certainly, much of our program will make its way to the church calendar. But what about those goals? Our ultimate goal, don't forget, is to help kids grow to be like the Lord. We need to break that down into smaller parts we can work on one at a time. Every child needs to understand the Gospel, so we need to introduce kids to the Lord. They need to learn how to live as Christians. They need to learn to pray. They must learn why obedience is best.

Your toolbox

This might be a good time to talk about what I call "the toolbox." Our home was destroyed by fire a couple of years ago; we lost almost everything. But my boys' bedroom furniture, simple stained wood coated in oil, survived the heat. (It was a shade darker afterwards, but we could still use it.) All I needed to do was sand the wood, apply new stain, and top it all off with a new coat of oil.

But I had no tools; they were all lost in the fire. So off to Sears I went, with a list in my pocket and a plan in my head. I would need a set of wrenches to take it apart and put it back together. I needed a new sander, lots of sandpaper, and a few smaller items to get the job done.

All of life is like that. Every job has its tools. As I write this book, I sit in front of my computer with a dictionary, almanac, and other "tools of the trade" nearby. When it's time to cut the grass, we get out the lawn mower. When the car has a flat, we open the trunk and find the jack. And when we help people grow in Christ, we use the tools God has provided.

Let's learn what these tools are all about.

Tool 1 - The Word of God

This is the one everybody guesses first. It certainly is the most important. The Bible is our number one tool to help kids grow in the Lord.

The night before Jesus died, He quietly knelt in the garden and prayed for all of us. He prayed that we would be protected from the attacks of Satan. He prayed that we might be unified in our love for Him and for each other. And He prayed that we might become holy like Him.

How was that to happen? Look carefully at Christ's prayer.

"Sanctify them through thy truth: thy word is truth"
(John 17:17).

When God sanctifies us He sets us apart for Himself and makes us holy. As we become holy, we become like His Son, Jesus Christ. Think back to our goal. Our main purpose is to fulfill God's purpose...that people might become like Christ. And Jesus knew that this happens as the Word of God does its work in our lives.

How can the Word of God work in children's lives? Be careful here. I'm an educated guy who is trained in the Book. Four years of Greek, a year of Hebrew, and almost 30 years of the King James Version have prepared me to look in the Bible and see what God has to say.

But the children in our churches aren't like that. One of the loudest cries of the Reformation was that the people of God must have the Word of God in their own language. But many faithful and revered translations in use today are not in the language of the children of your town!

I don't want to open a can of worms here, but I do want to make a suggestion. Encourage your children to own a Bible they can read themselves and understand. A doctrine close to our heart is that the Word of God can be understood by all Christians. People don't have to come to church to hear the official word as to what God has to say. Believers can look in their own Bibles and dig it out on their own.

So find a translation that your church will accept. My favorite is the New Century Version from Word Publishing. It is available as the International Children's Bible. Our entire family enjoys it for personal Bible study. But whatever one you choose, be sure it is one the children of your church will understand as they study it at home on their own.

Think about how many hours kids spend in church. If they average 3 hours a week, that adds up to over 2,000 hours before they leave high school. Think of what could be accomplished if every hour were planned! So be sure that your church program (Sunday School, Children's Church, and so on) takes advantage of every hour. We'll talk more about this in later chapters!

Tool 2 - *Learning Experiences*

God can use the successes and failures of our lives to help us grow to become like Christ. As you build relationships with the boys and girls of your town, you can be there when these good times and bad times come along. Your job is to help kids work through these situations to help them grow in Christ.

Times were tough during the early days of the Christian church. Jews who accepted Christ found that their new life was not well received back at home. So James, the Jewish Christian pastor of the first Church back at Jerusalem, wrote them a letter to get them back on track. He reminded them:

"...the trying of your faith worketh patience" (James 1:3).

James knew that the hard times they were facing could help them in their Christian growth. He didn't want them to miss the great lessons these days would bring.

I will always remember one particular Wednesday. Just before three o'clock that afternoon the kids filed through my office for their daily after-school cookie. Some used the phone, while others found a chair to sit and talk with their friends about the day. One tall 7th-grader came in and plopped in my lap as hard as he could while the other kids laughed at my groans of pain. But there was something the boy didn't know.

After his dad dropped him and his brother off at school that morning he had driven across town and carefully thought through what he was about to do. He withdrew money from the bank and bought a handgun and a little ammunition. Then he drove into a car wash, wrote a final note to his wife, and took his own life.

That evening I drove with a few men of the church to his home, praying that it wasn't true. Entering the home we found the reality of it all far more horrible than we could have imagined.

But I knew what I needed to do. I took the boys back into their room and let them talk. Then they both wrote a note to their dad I would read at his funeral several days later. We talked, we prayed, and I asked God to use this horrible day to make these boys more like Christ.

I remember another night. A busload of children returning from a visit to a Mexican mission camp was approaching the U.S. border. I had done this many times before and I knew what to expect. We would all be required to leave the bus and declare our citizenship as the customs officials searched the vehicle. But it was almost two in the morning, and I knew most of the kids couldn't even find their shoes, much less remember that they were Americans!

I don't know why I did it, but I took the microphone and led the children in a prayer that we might not even have to leave the bus. I knew that had never happened before, but I prayed that this one time it might happen for us tonight.

As we approached the customs building I gathered the birth certificates and found a waiting official to hear my story. I was bringing a busload of children from a missions trip. All were American children. The man instructed me to have the children leave the bus and enter that building. Inside, I groaned; this was not what we had wanted.

But seconds later a higher ranking official, seeing the first of the sleepy children leave the bus, came out and sent them back on. She came on the bus, heard our story, and in seconds we were on our way!

As we drove through the dark streets of Laredo, Texas, I took that microphone again and reminded the children that God had answered our most unusual prayer. This night was to have far greater impact than any Sunday School lesson I would ever teach on the subject. The Lord had taught a wonderful biblical truth to us through actual experience. He hears the prayers of His people!

So get yourself involved in the lives of some children. And be there when they make the all-star team, but also be there when their puppy dies. All of these times of happiness and tragedy can be used by the Lord to make us more like himself.

Tool 3 - Modeling

There is another tool we sometimes ignore that often is the most powerful of all. Rather than replace the Word of God, it illustrates it and makes it real and understandable.

When God wanted to reveal Himself to us He became a person. Jesus told us that:

"He that hath seen me hath seen the Father" (John 14:9).

The best way to understand God is to see Him in action in human flesh!

This is the very process Jesus Christ used to leave behind a team of men who were like him. Today it is called "modeling." It is an important truth we must understand in ministering to boys and girls.

Modeling: *People become like the people they spend time with whom they respect and admire.*

America is a culturally rich country, filled with the customs and ways of many people. How many different accents are spoken by people you know? Have you ever wondered how they developed?

As people came from other nations to live in America, they spoke their new language with the accents of their homelands. From these accents developed the countless American accents we recognize today. When we were little kids we learned them from the people around us.

We learn other things, too. We learn our prejudices, our traditions, and our feelings about Christ.

Jesus knew all about this. When He began His public ministry one of His first orders of business was to recruit some help. He would take these men and turn them into a trained team of professionals who would carry on the work after He was gone.

But look who He chose. One person seemed more interested in getting the Romans to leave town than in following Christ. Another was a moody guy who couldn't keep his mouth closed. Someone suggested that the only time Peter opened his mouth was to change feet! And Peter's brother, Andrew, seemed a bit on the quiet side. (Having spent his life around his brother, he probably never had the opportunity to talk much!) In short, this was certainly a motley group of men to be sent on such an important mission. But Jesus had a plan.

Mark explains that Jesus chose these men:

"They should be with him" (Mark 3:14).

The reason Jesus chose them was not because He was lonely and wanted someone around. Frankly, these guys weren't always that much company! But there was something else Jesus had in mind – a truth that can revolutionize our ministry with children if we fully understand what Jesus meant.

"The disciple is not above his master: but every one that is perfect shall be as his master" (Luke 6:40).

This is one of those verses that got lost in the translation! Let's look together at the New Century Version we noted earlier to see if we can better understand what Jesus was talking about.

"A student is not better than the teacher, but the student who has been fully trained will be like the teacher"
(Luke 6:40).

Jesus chose those twelve men that they might spend time with Him. In spending time with Him, they would become like Him!

This is one of the most amazing tools available to us. If we are like the Lord, and if we surround ourselves with kids who love and respect us, something wonderful will happen. They will become like us, and therefore become more like Christ!

But it works the other way, too! If we are impatient, our "disciples" will learn impatience. If we are easily discouraged, the kids in our class will become discouraged. But if our faith in God causes us to trust Him completely, the children with whom we minister will gradually see this faith growing in their lives – all because of a simple truth that grows out of the modeling process.

Christianity is caught as well as taught!

This kind of ministry takes time. But as the kids come to our homes, watch us in action, and see we are real, the truths God has taught us will be absorbed into their lives.

Growing in favor with man

We finally come to social relationships. I like to think of this part of the picture in several ways.

- I must teach children to obey God by respecting the authority structure He has created.

- I must help children learn to minister to other members of the body of Christ.
- I must train boys and girls to share their faith with their unsaved friends.

This process starts with learning to get along and share. Then it grows into a genuine Christian love for our brothers and sisters in Christ. Soon a love for the unsaved follows.

A part of the picture is teaching children good manners and how to act in front of others. We need to teach them how to stand up to peer pressure and how to stand alone. We must teach them that, in all their relationships with people, Christ must be honored.

The ministry is important. The plans are drawn and the tools are available to begin the job. There is no doubt about it: this is important business.

But still you wonder, "Am I the one? Can God use me for this work?"

Chapter One

REVIEW QUESTIONS:

1. What is our ultimate objective in ministering to children in the local church? Upon what Scripture is our objective based?

2. What are the four dimensions of church growth?

3. What tools has God provided for successful ministry?

DISCUSSION QUESTIONS:

1. What questions should we ask about our children's ministries that would help us discover the true value of each part of the program?

2. What are the implications of the significance of modeling in our ministries? How will this change the way we conduct ourselves and our programs?

3. How much involvement in a child's life is really necessary to accomplish the objectives outlined in this chapter? Is this level of involvement practical for a layperson? How do these truths apply to him or her?

Chapter Two

CAN GOD REALLY USE ME?

Chapter Two

CAN GOD REALLY USE ME?

Today I drove by his house. He doesn't live there anymore, though, because he's been with the Lord for several years. But I'll never forget what he did for me.

Mr. Drudge was quite old even then. To a 16-year-old almost everybody is old, but he was near retirement age and looked a lot older. Of all people, Mr. Drudge was the Senior High Sunday School teacher!

I wasn't a Christian yet, so I was never in his class. But that bowling activity one Tuesday night did it. All of his boys were there. One was my best friend who had invited me to come along. We bowled, we laughed, and we had a great time. Most important, this was my first exposure to Christians who loved the Lord. Another bowling activity followed. Next came that revival meeting where I met the Lord.

There was someone else even before Mr. Drudge. I was only five when my mom and dad took me to church. I can still visualize my first Beginner Department Sunday School class. I remember the little chairs and the take-home papers. I'll never forget the songs and the good feeling I had each time I walked into the room. But most of all, I remember Miss Estelle.

She was an older lady who thought little kids were great! I remember her telling my mom she was praying I would become a pastor. I didn't come to know the Lord until eleven years later. Then several years after that, the Lord answered her prayers.

God delights in using the most unlikely people. God can use one person's interest in sports and another's abilities in music. Most of all, God needs *willing hearts*.

God can use a proper role model

Remember the lesson of Luke 6:40? We become like
the people with whom we spend time – people whom we
respect and admire. The most important qualification
God is looking for is godliness...holy people who will do
what Jesus did, and live among people who will become
like them.

So don't worry if you're too old to play ball or your
voice is too weak to lead music. What you can do isn't
really all that important. Your strength as a children's
worker will come from what you are.

A boy in our church said something unusual at dinner one evening. "It will be a sad day when Herb Owen
dies," he announced to his parents. They agreed (I
think), but they wondered why he had said that. "Well,
he's holy and he's funny. And it's hard to find that com-
bination!"

God can use people who will use what they have

I hope your church will quickly get past the attitude
that every children's worker is a Sunday School teacher.
We all have different spiritual gifts to do lots of other
things in the church that need to be done, too.

Dan was a football coach until he lost his job. That
commonly happens to coaches, so he wasn't shocked. He
wasn't bitter, either. He had a few months on his hands
with nothing to do. So he came to me and volunteered
himself to lead our baseball league. He did an awesome
job! What a leader! And what a program!

Judy is an organizer. So when the kids choir
planned the dinner theater, she organized the kitchen
so the dinner went on without a hitch! There were signs
in many colors to help the volunteers understand just
what needed to be done. And her ministry was just as
important to the success of the evening as was the

choir's ministry. The successful dinner theater wouldn't have happened without her.

You would love Bob Johnson. He owns a farm and opens it to church groups to come for hikes and overnights and Bible studies. One day I was there with a group of kids. Lunch was almost ready. As Bob entered the building I asked him what we should do with the garbage. "You take care of the kids," he smiled. "I'll take care of the trash." His ministry was to help those who helped the kids. And I'll never forget him.

Terry was young, but even as a high school student he had the largest bus route of the church. Soon he became a leader in the Sunday night Bible clubs. Not long after, he came to see me about becoming a counselor at camp. The kids really loved him. He wasn't a "jock," and his musical talents were slight. But his tender and merciful heart drew boys and girls who needed his love. And love them he did!

Gordon Harper is a grandfather. In fact, several of his grandchildren live with him and his lovely wife, Betty. The Harpers love kids, and it is plain to see that the children of the church love them. Mr. Harper is a businessman...certainly not rich, but he knows how to handle money. I'll never forget the day he asked to meet me for lunch. He owned an empty building down the street and thought it would be a great place for a giant flea market. Gordon felt we could make at least a thousand dollars to pay for the new giant screen TV needed for Junior Church. I told him I didn't feel the church could sponsor it, so his daughter and several other ladies in the church did it on their own. I'll never forget the look on Clara Jones' face when she handed me the money we needed. Her dad knows how to spot a loose dollar for the Lord whenever he is near one, and his special gift from God was a help to us when we needed it most. He's helped countless others.

Gene taught accounting. He was the most organized man I knew. He was quiet and certainly would not be considered your typical children's worker. However, when we needed a 5th-grade teacher he was the man God sent along, so the class was his. And what a job he did! I had wondered if his college teaching experience would lead him to bore the kids with countless details about the Bible. But he was a dad himself — he knew how to do it. The class was well run, the awards were presented on time, and the man did a good job. And both the kids and their parents were grateful.

When I married Marilyn I knew I would be getting a great wife. But there was more in the package than the label revealed! Many times I've seen her sit down with a mom and daughter, and help them work through their problems. She knows just how to help each person see what she needs to do to grow in the Lord. And ladies often stop her in the halls to ask for help with a problem at home or with a discouragement that needs some encouragement.

Do you know about Jack Wyrtzen? The Word of Life ministries he founded are amazing. The facilities are lovely and the programs are the best in the world. But that's not really what makes his ministries shine. Every time Jack speaks he tells a thrilling story of another young life who met Christ. In fact, my wife trusted the Lord as a child at a Word of Life Rally where Jack spoke in Peoria, Illinois. This man of God has a burden to win the young people of the world to Christ. A lot of church leaders care about youth in general. Jack is burdened for kids...specific young people who hear the Gospel from his very lips. And it wasn't until he was well past the age of 60 that I ever even thought about his age. A love for people is timeless, and age just doesn't make a difference. Any person who brings souls to Christ will always find an open ear and heart, ready to hear a message from God.

I will never forget the night I knew God wanted me to pastor children. I knew what I wanted to do, but I had never heard of anyone who pastored just boys and girls. Pastoring children? Whoever heard of that? But I found a large church that would give me a chance to try out my ideas. I got busy and went to work, doing what I knew to do as I learned even more day by day. I soon found lots of little sheep who needed a shepherd. I didn't want to replace their moms and dads; I wanted to help them. I wanted to teach the Bible on a level kids could understand. I wanted to be there when they needed someone to talk to. I wanted to organize and plan programs to help the kids become like Christ. And I found that God had a place for me.

So it really is true: God can use everybody. And God can use you.

- Dan isn't a Sunday School teacher, but he is a coach. Our sports program blossomed because of his *leadership*.

- Judy is an *organizer*. Whenever a big project comes along, it is done first class.

- Mr. Bob Johnson is always in the background because he loves to *help* those who help people.

- Terry has a heart full of *mercy*. Today he is on his way to the mission field to work with the children of Mexico.

- Gordon Harper can quickly help bring a project to completion because of his abilities to *use money* to do God's work.

- Gene is a *teacher* who can help kids understand the facts of the Bible.

- Marilyn is an *exhorter*, and her words of encouragement can help build up a discouraged mom to take hold of her family.

- *Evangelist* Jack Wyrtzen is responsible for more young people hearing the Gospel than perhaps any other man of our century.

- And the Lord has allowed me to *pastor* thousands of children and help them grow in the Lord.

All of these faithful people have found great satisfaction in using their spiritual gifts to serve God.[1]

You may be a lot like one of these people. I've known a lot of people who *wouldn't* do anything for the Lord, but I've never met one who *couldn't* if he or she would use the talents and spiritual gifts the Lord provided for winning and training boys and girls for Christ.

God can use people who will build relationships with children to help mold and direct their lives

My first pastor was a quiet man. The church was small and the organization problems were relatively simple. So when I became a Christian, my pastor was able to spend his time with me. Every Tuesday he picked up me and some friends and took us to the YMCA for swimming lessons. On Saturdays he took me on errands and explained his work to me. He was one of only a few my mom invited to my high school graduation party. I would not be here today if he had not been there then.

What changed my life was not that Glenn Pace was my pastor, but that he was my friend. To this day I am grateful for his friendship and the time he invested in me. What he did for me I, in return, have done for lots of others. And it is worth the effort.

Tim called last night. He moved to Michigan just after he finished sixth grade. It was a tearful good-bye. But he came back to visit for the summer a year or two later and still writes and calls to tell me what's going on.

His dad had moved to our town to go to school, leaving Tim with lots of time on his hands. When we moved into our new home, Tim was there to help me paint the basement. And when the teachers decided he'd best repeat sixth grade, they all decided I should tell him. Now Tim is a student at a nearby Bible college. He has received the benefit of lots of caring people, and at college he will grow through the ministry of many more. All the while he, himself, is becoming a tool in God's hands, ready to pass on to others what he has received himself.

Relationships take time to build. If you are a Sunday School teacher, pick up a couple of kids when you go to the grocery store or to the mall. Take some to the ball game and spend an evening at their games. Invite them over for hamburgers or pizza. And invite their families over to build relationships. Why? Remember what we learned about modeling? It is one of the greatest tools available to make the truths of Scripture live in the eyes of boys and girls.

I would not be the person I am today if godly people were not there when I was young and still a new believer. As we grow in Christ we find we need a mentor, an older brother or sister in Christ who can direct us in places he or she has gone before.

God uses Gospel tracts, workbooks, and videotapes. He can use music, audiocassettes, and hard times to bring people closer to Himself. But He usually prefers to use real people, flesh and blood embodiments of the love He has shared with the world.

Think of all the technology the recent years has brought us. The age of the electronic church has made its way to Sunday School, where week after week dedicated Christian musicians play the latest instruments of praise to God.

To be successful in ministering to children, however, you must remember that the most important tool is *yourself* – living with and living for the kids to whom you minister. In *Christian Education: Seeking to Become Like Jesus Christ* (Grand Rapids, Michigan: Zondervan Publishing House, 1975), Larry Richards explains seven important factors that must be present in the teaching/learning process of discipleship and modeling. I often simplify them in this way:

Seven Secrets of Successful Modeling and Discipleship

1. There must be frequent and long-term contact between you and the child whose life you want to touch. Sundays alone just will not do it.

2. There must be a warm, loving relationship between you and your "disciple." You love each other, and both of you know it.

3. Your "disciple" must see you as you really are, and come to know the real you.

4. Your "disciple" must see you in a variety of life settings and situations. This will take more than an hour on the Lord's Day. You are going to include this person in your life, not just in your Sundays.

5. You must live a consistent life before your "disciple," while clearly exhibiting in your life what you believe and teach.

6. What you live must be consistent with the teachings of your church family.

7. You must explain to your "disciple" why you do what you do, and use experiences you share together as teaching times to illustrate what you believe.

God can use you if you will be available to Him. I remember when the pastor asked my mom to teach first-grade Sunday School.

"I can't do that. I don't know the Bible well enough. I'm not a teacher..."

And on the reasons went. Somehow she took the class. For almost ten years she was there every Sunday morning. She loved those little girls, and they loved her. She still delights in telling stories about those kids. Many of them probably remember her, too. Mom would get her book and her Bible, and would learn more than she needed to feed those hungry hearts on Sunday. Then she would come back for more so she'd have more to share the next Sunday.

Thank the Lord He wants you! And thank Him that those children need you. Decide where you can help and give it all you have!

---

[1]For a fuller explanation of spiritual gifts and their role in accomplishing God's work, read *Team Ministry: Finding Meaning and Fulfillment through Understanding the Spiritual Gift within You*, by Larry Gilbert, available from Church Growth Institute.

Chapter Two

REVIEW QUESTIONS:

1. What are the three characteristics of people God can use?

2. What nine spiritual gifts are represented by the workers mentioned in this chapter?

3. What are Richards' principles of discipleship?

DISCUSSION QUESTIONS:

1. Which one of the spiritual gifts we discussed most closely describes your desire to serve the Lord? What does this tell you about how God can use you in children's ministries?

2. What are some ways that you, in your present situation, can build relationships with children to help them grow in Christ? How do we include the child's parents in these relationships?

3. Why is consistency in our Christian lives important? Does it matter what we do when children are not around? Why? Or why not?

Chapter Three

GOALS FOR YOUR MINISTRY

Chapter Three

GOALS FOR YOUR MINISTRY

We have talked a lot about goals in our ministry. Someone said that a person who does not know where he is going probably will never get there. Let's review what we've learned so far about our objectives in ministry.

OUR ULTIMATE GOAL
- To help children become like Christ
  Romans 8:29

THE DIMENSIONS OF OUR MINISTRY
- Mental growth in wisdom
- Physical growth to serve God
- Spiritual growth to know the Lord
- Social growth to minister to people
  Luke 2:52

OUR TOOLS IN MINISTRY
- The Word of God
  John 17:17
- Learning Experiences
  James 1:3
- Modeling
  Mark 3:14; Luke 6:40

Let's talk more about how we can practically implement our goals in daily ministry.

Helping children develop character

As you begin to work with your Sunday School class, your basketball team or your club group, you will soon notice that there are many different kinds of children in that room. Some are so obedient you wonder if they are human. Others will try you a little, while even others have no idea that you are in charge. Then there are the noisy ones, the ones who ask a thousand questions, the ones who don't seem to hear anything you say, and the ones who catch every mistake you make. Some like to sing, while others think music is for sissies. What a crew you have in there! How can you possibly meet the needs of all these children?

Begin by remembering why you are there. You want to help these children become more like Christ. Some do not know the Lord, and your first goal for them is easy to determine. Others are in various stages of Christian growth, complicated by differing temperaments and backgrounds.

Growing in the Lord can be defined in terms of Christian character. We usually think of "character" as doing right and remaining true to important principles. That idea is not too far from what we have in mind, but there is more. Character must be understood in the light of our ultimate goal of Christlikeness. If we could come up with a list of specific character goals it would then be easier to help children grow to reach them.

In other words, I want my children to become like Jesus. In studying the life of Christ we discover specific qualities of His life that we should duplicate in our lives. From this thought comes our definition of character.

Character
The qualities of my life which, in their perfection, are the qualities of Jesus Christ's life.

If we want to become like Jesus we need to find out what Jesus was like. Here is a suggestion for your future devotional Bible study.

- Read carefully through the four gospels.

- In your reading search for specific things that Christ did and taught that show you what He is like.

- From your study define the character qualities we want God to reproduce in our lives and in the lives of our children.

- Create projects for each of your children (as well as for yourself) to help these qualities grow in their lives.

This project has some prerequisites. You will need to know your children well. You will also need to take time to know Jesus Christ and grow in your understanding of the life He lived on earth.

Each time you are with your children, carefully notice what is happening in their lives. Don't just lament their problems. Recognize conflicts in their behavior as symptoms of deeper needs where God wants you to help. If they never had problems in class or on the team you would not know they existed.

Helping children develop character begins with a study of the life of Christ and continues as you transfer what you learned into their lives.

An example from my own Bible study notes is shown on the next page.

Jesus in the garden

What is the text?	"And he went a little farther, and fell on his face, and prayed, saying, O my Father, if it be possible, let this cup pass from me: nevertheless not as I will, but as thou wilt" (Matt. 26:39).
What did Christ do?	• He obeyed His father in spite of the suffering He knew would be involved. • He accepted the death of the Cross, knowing that resurrection Sunday would follow and He would live again.
What in Christ's life should be reproduced in my life?	• Obedience - Doing what God wants me to do, whatever the cost. • Faith - Believing what God said, even if I can see nothing now that shows me it is true.
How can I help my children develop these qualities in their lives?	**Julian** - Because he has trouble obeying I want to help him develop an obedient spirit. • Ask Julian to play the lead in the Sunday School play about Noah's obedience before an unbelieving world. • While helping him with his part, discuss how difficult it must have been for Noah to obey God while nobody else would. Discuss Julian's struggles in obedience, and pray with him about his needs. • Help Julian list the conflicts he feels in disobeying the authorities God has placed over him. • List measurable goals to help him understand how he is doing in working toward the goal of obedience. • Schedule weekly accountability meetings with him to measure his progress and offer support and encouragement.

A wise children's worker will look at every contact with children as another opportunity to help them in the process of growing to become like Christ. We need to understand their needs and have solutions ready from the Word of God. Just throwing a few verses at the problem will never solve it. Our lives can illustrate the Scriptural principles and be used by God to help change lives.

Helping children grow toward spiritual independence

Babes in Christ need to grow. My family and I recently spent several weeks helping missionaries in Mexico. During our visits over the years we have come to understand their strategy.

- A team moves into a new village and begins to form relationships with the people.

- These relationships soon lead to the local people making observations of the lifestyles of the believers.

- The local people are invited to Bible studies that explain that these are not the ways of Americans, but rather the ways of Christians.

- One by one, some of the people begin to accept Christ and begin a lifetime of discipleship.

- A church is formed of the new believers.

- As the spiritual gifts and spiritual maturity of the new believers becomes evident, it becomes clear that God has called some for special places of spiritual leadership.

- These growing leaders receive special training and are given places of service.

- As these new leaders grow, they take their places of service in the church, and soon one becomes the pastor.

- The church leadership is now made up of local believers who infiltrate their village and begin the process again within the church.

- The missionary team moves on to another village
  and begins a ministry with new people.

The work of a missionary closely parallels the work
of a children's worker in a local church. We want to help
our children grow in the Lord until they don't need us
anymore, or at least not in the same way they used to
need us. When our ministry in their lives is finished,
God will send someone else along to carry on the work.
Then as they grow, our "kids" will influence people and
begin a ministry of their own.

I met one special boy when he was entering the
third grade. His family had disintegrated under the
worse possible circumstances, and he had come to live
with his grandparents who were seeking help as they
began again in their parenting roles.

I spent a lot of time with him. We laughed and
played together. We discussed the problems of his family. I did my best to help him absorb and accept it all.
Later he came under the influence of high school leaders
who continued to meet his needs. Soon he was the self-
appointed evangelist at his high school, working in Bible
clubs and leading prayer meetings. As His stand for
Christ was clear (perhaps sometimes a little too bold,
but his influence was clearly felt), God used his life to
plant the seeds of conviction of sin in the lives of others.

Thinking through his life in the years that I have
known him, I appreciate the amazing growth that has
occurred in his life as countless people met his needs,
discipled him, and held him accountable for his life before God.

A plan of action

What are some specific things we can do to help children grow toward spiritual independence?

- **Help them develop regular habits of Bible study.** A Christian is prepared to live for Christ, wherever he/she may be, if he/she knows to go directly to the source for direction and instruction.

- **Teach them to pray.** An evangelist used to define prayer simply as "asking" and the answer to prayer as "receiving." It is important that children learn to go to God for their needs.

- **Teach them to obey.** A submissive spirit is of primary importance and is, perhaps, the key to Christian growth.

- **Teach them to stand alone.** Children need to be prepared for peer pressure and the world's demands that try to conform them to the world.

- **Teach them to live their lives by conviction, not by circumstance.** The Christian is to make basic decisions of commitment to Christ that control all of his future actions. If a child's self-worth is established by wise parents and church leaders, he will not need the approval of friends to validate his worth. He will then be able to reject temptations to follow the poor leadership of unworthy heroes.

Although you many never see the final result of your ministry in the lives of very many children, you will begin to see some changes. You will see your some of your boys and girls begin to develop habits of godliness that will aid them in their lifelong journey of growing in the Lord.

Building strong families

One of the results of a successful ministry to children is the development of stronger Christian families.

It is not enough that children try to go it alone. Children
need a complete family structure of mutual support and
commitment to Christ that helps each member grow in
the Lord. Let me provide some suggestions.

1. Get to know the families of your children.

When you visit the kids at home, find out all you can
about their home life. Are the parents Christians? Is
there a mom and a dad? What help does this family
need? Discover these needs and offer to help. Invite the
family to your home for dinner and show them what a
strong Christian family looks like.

I can hardly believe I have forgotten her name, but I
will never forget what one girl said. She was only a
sixth-grader, but she was obviously in love with the
ways of the world. The other girls were in love with her.
Her bad influence was one of the strongest challenges I
ever faced at that church. One day I found out why.

Marilyn and I were newlyweds. We often invited
kids over for dinner. One day this particular girl was
helping with the dishes when those horrible words
came. "My mom told me to never get married, and never
have children!" I never found out what happened to this
girl but could almost guess. I wish I could have helped
her family. I wish we could have done something more
to help that girl.

Remember this figure: over 25% of all children live
with only one parent. Those homes are going to need
some help. In your area the percentage may be higher. I
remember an apartment complex where 17 boys attended our church club; only one had a dad, and he
wasn't much of one at that.

Find out what these families are really like. Learn
what individual help they need, and offer to be there to
provide help to get these families moving toward suc-

cess. This may be the most important thing you do for their children.

2. Offer parenting classes.

Both strong and weak families know they need some help. Why not have classes to train them in the basic principles of parenting? Our culture requires extensive training and documentation of success to drive a car, teach school or even be a lifeguard at the neighborhood pool. There are no such requirements for being a parent. There are lots of folks out there who just do not know what they are doing. Failing parents produce children who are failures too. These folks need our help.

Marilyn and I just completed a year of Tuesday morning classes for the moms in our church. It was part of a preexisting ladies fellowship program. Some were fine mothers who could have taught the class as well as we did. Others were struggling in more basic ways. But all needed encouragement. Everybody said it was a highlight of their week.

Why not schedule a weekly class in the recreation building at a local apartment project? You are not having church, so there shouldn't be much to scare the management and unbelieving tenants away. But you are going to share scriptural principles, and will therefore lead many to the Lord.

Visit your local bookstore. There you will find many good Bible study guides and books to help you train others. Bring testimonies from other successful parents and from those who have struggled and found help. Parents need to know that they are not the only ones who want support and that their families are not the only ones under pressure. They need to understand that the Lord can help and that the Bible is filled to the brim with wonderful principles and truths that can revolutionize their homes.

3. Become a resource center of help to families.

People are looking for places where things are happening. While we understand that God can meet their needs, we also understand that He is manifested through His people as they assemble to worship and to minister. As you become a source of help to children and families, you will soon discover that the word is out and people will be drawn in for help. Be always willing to meet the needs of families, even if they are not associated with your church.

4. Go after dads.

Throughout the Bible God expresses His concern that fathers be godly leaders of their homes. What do you remember about Abraham? His faith, of course, was held in high esteem throughout Scripture as an example for us all. But something else stands out in my mind. What else did God say about this great man?

*"I know him, that he will command his children
and his household after him,
and they shall keep the way of the Lord"* (Gen. 18:19).

A godly dad is the best insurance against a disintegrating family. I used to lead a monthly fathers' breakfast on Saturday mornings. One of the dads was a chef, and those morning meals were great. But the fellowship was even grander.

I would share principles from the Bible, then we would allow the men to share their own struggles and testimonies of success. The finest fathers were usually the most sensitive to their own needs. That shocking revelation stirred self-examination as well. So do something for the dads of your kids, and invite them to bring others. Not only will you reach new families that way, but you'll also see amazing things begin to happen among the homes you already touch.

We will expand on these goals and offer others in later chapters. I hope you are beginning to see that your job is bigger than absorbing the lesson one evening and squeezing it out again on Sunday morning. I never cease to be amazed at the influence we can have on children, and on the families that know we care about their kids. If we use this influence to their good, much will happen that will have eternal results. And the amazing part of it all is that God chose to use us!

Chapter Three

REVIEW QUESTIONS:

1. Define Christian character. How can we learn of Christ's character?

2. What strategy do missionaries to Mexican villages follow to win and disciple the local people? How does it relate to your ministry?

3. What five things should be a part of a child's life as he or she grows in Christian maturity toward spiritual independence?

DISCUSSION QUESTIONS:

1. What ministries of a local church could have been a great help to your family when you were a child? What would have been the results of a powerful ministry in your life? If your family was part of such a ministry, how did the Lord use this ministry in your family?

2. How would you characterize the greatest character need of modern children? How should we respond to this need?

3. What are the greatest sources of stress faced by modern families? How should local churches respond to help families withstand these pressures?

Chapter Four

HOW CAN I REACH NEW CHILDREN?

Chapter Four

HOW CAN I REACH NEW CHILDREN?

I have heard of it happening to others. I am glad it happened to me...

I had picked up some kids and a worker in the next little town, and we were on our way to a ball game in the city. Driving down the area's main street I noticed something rather strange happening right before my eyes. Hundreds of people were lined up along the road as if they were waiting for something great to happen. Then, one by one, many began to wave at me. Why were they there? What was going on?

Suddenly it all became clear. This was the night of the big parade in the little town. These waving kids were from our church. They recognized me and wanted to say "hello." The other people in the crowd didn't know that, so they began to wave as well! They must have thought we were the first unit in the parade and this was a car full of somebody important!

That's when it happened. All of those faces were looking at me. I began to look back. Lots of kids whom I knew were there, but so were hundreds of boys and girls I did not know. I found myself wondering, do they know the Lord? Why haven't we met them and invited them to church. We were the largest church in the area and over 200 4th-, 5th- and 6th-graders attended each week. Here at the parade, those we knew were outnumbered by those we did not know. Some of them must have known the Lord. There were other good churches around doing the job and reaching people for Christ. But somehow I knew I was looking into the faces of many more who were like sheep without a shepherd – people who needed Christ.

Maybe you have felt that way. Perhaps you have wondered, "How can I reach some of these kids for Christ? Is there something I can do?" The following suggestions have worked for many other burdened children's workers just like you.

Be where the kids are

The best way to reach children is to build relationships with them. Sometimes this will mean accepting positions of authority over children so they and their parents will look to you for direction. Once they know you care about them, your opportunities for ministry and evangelism begin to grow. Here are some specific suggestions.

- Coach a team. You should consider developing a sports program to provide the needs of your church kids as well as to reach others. If that isn't possible, get involved in an existing league in your city. Pray that God will send lots of kids to you who need the Lord and your help and guidance.

- Be a volunteer at school functions. Kids learn to like the teacher's aide and the game director at field day. Be there to become a part of their lives.

- Go to their school plays. Never miss a special event when a child invites you if you can possibly go. In addition to assuring the child of your love, you will meet lots of little friends who need Christ.

- Help in any way you can. I have taken sound systems, set them up and run them for school plays. I've conducted choir workshops at public schools and offered to go along on field trips to help; anything to be seen by children and to build relationships with them.

The more baited lines in the water, the more fish you will catch. The more relationships you build, the more children you will reach. It's just that simple. If you will learn to gently use every relationship, not in a forceful insensitive way, but in a gentle manner, you will reach children.

Plan special promotions

We've somehow changed it all around. The church was meant to be the place where Christians gather for worship and fellowship. The world was where the unsaved were to be found. And the church was to go into the world with the Gospel.

However, that's not how it usually works. We have opened the doors of the church and, as they say in the South, loudly proclaimed, "Y'all come!" But this is America – and many parts of our nation have a Christian heritage. Sometimes those who aren't Christians will come if there is something worth coming to.

I knew a man with a boat. (Everybody ought to know a man with a boat.) He willingly agreed to give rides on the river one Sunday afternoon to anyone I would bring. So I promoted it big, found a man in the church to drive the kids, and recruited a cook to provide lunch. Then I waited to see what would happen.

We averaged about 30 participants in our class on any given week, plus 20 visitors came that day. That's 50 for the boat. Did he say boat or yacht? I couldn't remember.

Fortunately, we had planned a bus (not a van) to get the boys to the river that afternoon. The good captain had a great sense of humor. He thought a big crowd was just fine! So we took several trips and found other activities for those waiting their turn. It was a wonderful afternoon. But the most important part was the several kids who decided that if church was like this, they would be back! And they did come back...week after week...and many of them trusted the Lord.

Special days do work. Consider carefully the kids you want to reach and what it would take to reach them. You cannot build your ministry on special promotions, but they do put you in contact with new people so you can form those all-important relationships that will lead to eternal fruit.

We rented Putt-Putt and invited kids to invite their friends. We conservatively figured out how many might come and divided the cost among them. Lots of kids did come, and each one filled out the registration card that provided us with further information.

REGISTRATION CARD

Name _____

Address _____

City _____ State _____ Zip _____

Phone _____ Birthdate_____

School_____ Grade _____

Church you attend _____

Names of all parents with whom you live_____

_____

_____

This card contains all of the information needed to further follow up on the child. Never have an activity or service without a supply of these cards on hand. And make a computer file from these cards for mailings and further follow-up.

Regularly schedule special activities

You may visit the home of the best friend of a child in your church, act friendly, and show Christian love.

Then you innocently invite the boy to Sunday School. The mother's response is almost a reflex: "We have our church."

That would be the end of it all if you didn't have another plan. Always have scheduled an upcoming special activity to which you can invite new kids. I usually try to get a child to visit a special activity before I invite him to church. The child has been with us, his family knows us, and they are less likely to refuse your invitation.

Unlike the activities we discussed in the previous section, these activities are not related to Sunday School attendance. A trip to a major league ball game, a camping trip, a three-hour bowling tournament or a day at the skating rink will bring out lots of visitors. Prepare printed information that clearly states where the activity will be, what is involved, when it starts, and when it ends. If you are leaving on the church bus from the parking lot, always leave no earlier than five minutes after the announced time. And never return late. The longer parents wait in a dark parking lot the madder they become.

Activities must be well-planned, well-chaperoned, and lots of fun. Look in the phone book and in the newspaper for ideas if your thinker runs a little dry. Be aware that kids want to do some things only once. They will do other things once a month.

Once I announced a hike along the Appalachian Trail in Shenandoah National Park. The teens would go on Tuesday, and the juniors would follow on Thursday. I found a dad with the day off to drive the bus, recruited a few other parents to go along, and thought all was fine. I even met with the teens the Sunday night before to tell them all about it.

I was a better salesman than I thought. Over 80 kids showed up on Tuesday morning, including girls in high heels who had no idea what they were getting into. We started late because I had to round up another bus driver. And the hike itself...was a classic. One girl tripped and sprained her ankle to add to the fun. We cut down several small trees to make supports for a stretcher. I won't describe the rest of the day, but it was certainly memorable.

But the kids came. And they filled out those registration cards. When I took the hike with the juniors on Thursday we picked up trash left by the big guys two days before. Unlike the teens, not one junior griped about a thing. And they couldn't believe how beautiful the mountains were. The teens had, somehow, failed to notice that. (Looking back, I think this was the very day I decided the Lord had called me to children's work.) More importantly, each child was registered and each one had a great day!

Plan a DU every now and then. A Destination Unknown can be lots of fun because the kids never know what is coming up next. (Tell the parents they can call as soon as the bus leaves for information if they want to know what is going on.) Once we announced a day like this and it went great. We started with a quick hike along a brook, spent 16 minutes at a beautiful playground, bowled a game, went for the food bar at a restaurant with great kids' menu prices, visited the city visitors center and watched the welcome video, and went to the Dollar Store (we provided the dollars). The day cost the kids $5 and they loved it. And it only cost the church the price of the gas for the bus.

Plan a summer camp

Nothing has proved more effective in reaching new kids and building your regulars than a great summer camp program. I have seen hundreds of campers won to Christ who later became involved in a local church.

Good books are available to help you. And if you announce your program well enough in advance, you will be sure to find lots of free volunteer help.

Conserve the results

Whatever you do, be sure your church becomes known as the "kids place" in your town. And once they come, what are you going to do with all these names?

Visit them. Put them on your mailing list. Pray for them. Make them a part of your ministry.

Steve and Kimberly had a friend who had seen the world. Club Med had a camp. Steve's friend wanted him and his sister to go along. But Steve's mom wasn't about to go for that. So Steve thought and came up with an alternative. A large church in town (our church) had a camp. Why couldn't he and his sister go to this camp instead?

So they came. And they loved it. They went home and told Mom and Dad all about it!

Now you need to understand Steve's mom to follow this next part. (She's the Judy who organized the dinner theater for the kids choir.) When her kids are involved, she wants to know what is going on. So the entire family came to the church and they liked it, too!

Before long the kids were involved, the family was teaching Sunday School, and they were all bringing others to hear the Gospel. It all started with camp.

Remember how I became a Christian? It started with a bowling activity planned by the senior high boys Sunday School class at a small church. Now here I am. I have repeated the process to reach hundreds of children like someone reached me. It's your turn.

Chapter Four

REVIEW QUESTIONS:

1. What are five secrets that will help you reach new children?

2. What are four ways you can be where the kids are?

3. How can the regular use of registration cards help you reach children?

DISCUSSION QUESTIONS:

1. How can relationships help you reach children?

2. What kind of summer camp program would accomplish the most in helping you reach and disciple children in your church? What would be your goals? What kind of program would you plan?

3. Think about the area where you live and minister. What kind of activities could you plan, using the facilities available nearby?

Chapter Five

VISITING IN THE HOMES
OF CHILDREN

Chapter Five

VISITING IN THE HOMES OF CHILDREN

The roast is on the table, the rolls are out of the oven, and the family is about to sit down for dinner. DING-DONG. That was the doorbell. You go to the door and there stands a salesman of cemetery plots. I don't think he is going to get in.

When you make a call, things can turn out the same way for you unless you plan your visit in advance. Early in my ministry I went along on a lot of fruitless trips because of some important principles I did not know. I knew to pray before going, but had not learned some other needed advice.

7 Basic Principles for a Successful Visit

The old saying reminds us, "If we fail to plan, we plan to fail." Successful visits don't just happen. Anyone who has visited others at all has learned a lot of things that just don't work. But what does work? Here are seven suggestions that can turn potentially wasted evenings into times of great success.

1. *Clearly understand your objectives.*

If you don't know why you are going you won't know what to do when you get there. What do you really want to accomplish? Why are you going?

- Is this a first contact where you want to build trust?

- Is this family ready to hear a presentation of the Gospel?

- Has the child been absent?

- Is there a problem with which you may be able to help?

- Do you want the child to become more involved?

- Are there behavior problems that need to be discussed?

- Are the parents upset with a problem that developed?

- Can this family be recruited as workers in the ministry?

Each of your potential goals calls for a well thought-out plan. Think through the various things that might happen, and the different things that might possibly be said. Have your response ready, thought out ahead of time, so you can better meet the needs of the family.

Work to build trust. If you want to build the confidence of the family, help them know who you are and how much you care for their children.

Carefully consider the family's spiritual background. Then you will know best when and how to present the Gospel.

Be discreet in responding to the parents' reasons why a child may have been absent. This family is probably operating with a different set of priorities than you are. Never make them feel guilty because the child was not at church. Work toward the future.

You can help every family. We will talk more about looking for ways you can meet a need of every family. The more you know about these people the better job you will do.

Carefully discern how quickly you can suggest further involvement in your ministry. I became a Christian one Tuesday night and was ready for Sunday School the following Lord's Day. It was not until a few weeks later that I learned I could come on Sunday evening too! I was ready for anything they would print in the bulletin, and Mom and Dad were thrilled. Other families might be frightened by such a sudden absorption of their child into the program of the church. Will family times be neglected? Will homework suffer? Is the child already heavily involved in other activities? Think through these things before you visit.

Do not be afraid to tell parents how their children are behaving. Assure them you are on their side. I have often used well-planned words to let parents know there is a problem. "I know you are a good mother and would want to know about this." In saying these words you take the side of the parents, letting them know you do not think the behavior of the child is a reflection on the family. Parents may often be quick to offer further information to help you understand their children's needs. The actions of a child with physical or emotional disabilities will be interpreted differently once you understand.

Never defend yourself. You may often feel threatened when a parent complains about something or is angry because of what happened (or what was perceived as happening) at church. Listen carefully to the parents' concerns without interrupting, and assure them you understand how they feel. Honestly admit mistakes you or a worker may have made, apologize for them and show the parent how you will make certain this will never happen again. If the parents' anger resulted from a misunderstanding, gently explain what happened from your perspective. Never allow a parent to feel foolish because of his or her rash words.

Help the parents see how their gifts can be used in your ministry. People will often respond with a list of what they cannot do while failing to see how God has equipped them for service. In a growing church there is something everybody can do to help in the work of God.

2. Make an appointment.

Like the cemetery plot salesman, you will not get in either, if it is a bad time for company. So call in advance. Tell the parents who you are, that you're from the church, and you'd like to come by and say "Hi!" If the time you have planned does not suit, ask for another time that would be better.

Be flexible in your visitation. Go after dinner but before bedtime for the kids. Saturdays may be good. During the day may work during the summer. So ask the family what would be the best time for your visit. Adjust your schedule so you can call at a more convenient hour.

"But if I just drop by won't there be an element of surprise?" Yes, there probably will. And that is just what you are trying to avoid. Think about your own home. People drop by unexpectedly and the lady of the house looks around, decides the place is a mess and apologizes for it all the whole time you are there. It does not make for a very pleasant experience.

Here is a list of potential advantages of calling in advance to make sure it is okay to come.

- You do not waste a visit to an empty house.
- Because they know you are coming, the lady of the house has time to make the living room presentable, and is not embarrassed by your being there.
- Everyone you want to see will likely be at home.
- The family is mentally prepared for your visit. You will get more done this way.
- You might even get a hot slice of apple pie before you leave!

"Does this mean I never visit without an appointment?" No, there will be times it will be okay to make a brief, unannounced visit. Once people become your friends you will know what to do. Sometimes you can visit at the door when you are returning a child home after a church activity or when dropping off something for the family. After a while you will learn to find excuses to make "unplanned" visits.

When I was unmarried, I quickly took note of the available ladies at the church where I ministered. I learned that one lovely young lady was already interested, and that she would be more than happy to play the piano in Junior Church the next Sunday. So I naturally thought it my duty to drop the music by while I was "in the neighborhood." Not only did she agree to play the piano, but a year later she agreed to become my wife. I assure you there were lots of other planned visits in the "follow-up" process!

I have often remembered what I learned that night. And I have made lots of "I just wanted to drop this by" visits that were short and included only conversations filtered through the screen door. But if you expect to get inside, be sure to call ahead. People will appreciate your thoughtfulness. They will recognize your consideration for their personal needs. And you will definitely get more done.

3. Visit the family, not just the child.

People who do not know you do not want you talking to their kids alone. If you really want an effective ministry, your concern for the child must include the family, too. Include everyone in your visit; you will quickly discover great things beginning to happen.

- The family will see that you are interested in each of them.

- You will learn more about the needs of the family and how their interaction affects the child.

- You will earn the trust of the family, making deeper ministry more possible.

• You will discover needs, problems, and opportunities you would have otherwise missed.

I always make it a policy to ask the child if I can see his room. (If the mother shrieks in horror and I discern this probably is not a good time, I'll skip it.) This part of the visit lets the child know I think he or she is special, and tells me a lot about his or her interests. A room full of C. S. Lewis books tells me one thing about the child. Rock star posters on the wall tell me something else. Visiting the child's room provides me with important information I can later use to help the entire family.

4. Explain what you can do for the child and the family.

All good salespeople understand this important principle. If you want to make a sale you must look for a need the buyer has that you can meet, even if the buyer has never realized the need exists!

A little girl who visited our church lived in a duplex not too far away. One evening a worker and I stopped by (after calling for an appointment). The mother was pleased that her little girl had a good time at church. I soon realized there was no dad around, and these folks did not have a lot of money. As we talked together, my friend and I took mental note of everything we saw, everything we heard. We wanted to do something to meet a need of this lady so we could begin a broader ministry to her family. Once that ministry began we would work to lead this family to Christ.

Then the mom said the magic words. Before she could begin her new job she would need to complete two weeks of evening classes at the community college. She had no car and didn't know how she would get there. That was my opportunity.

I told her I would be glad to take care of her transportation needs, and she willingly gave me all the details. She needed to be there at 7:00 p.m., so I told her to be ready at 6:40. It would be over at 9:00, so I noted that as well. As we were leaving I told her I would call her before her classes began to tell her who would pick her up. I assured her not to worry about a thing, and she assured me the little girl would be back the next Sunday morning!

Well, I didn't have the slightest idea how she was going to get there, either. But I went to work on it – and the church ladies fellowship saved the day! This good visit began a relationship that would help us help that family.

There are many other ways to reach children and families. Our church children's choir was well-known around town. Many people in town had heard about the kids, and I often invited new children to visit and join. I also kept one of our cassettes and a video in the car if they needed to know more. We reached a lot of children that way.

At one church where I ministered we planned a sports program with something for everybody. We started in the fall with soccer, then in late October the older children moved on into flag football. Basketball leagues played all winter, and in the spring we began tee ball for the primaries, softball for the junior girls, and baseball for the guys. We even had a wrestling program for a while. Occasionally we had the local Christian college sponsor a track meet for us. When visiting sports-minded families we often used the sports program to begin relationships that would lead to reaching a family for Christ.

Once I visited a family of several sharp kids who seemed to have it made. They all did well in school and loved the band and chorus; they were all involved in the community sports leagues; and this was a family of fine, decent folks. From their prospective they did not need our children's choir or our sports program, and they certainly did not need Jesus Christ.

Then I said the magic word: *camp*. We owned a 36-acre island that was home to a simply awesome facility and a full summer program. Lights went on all over the place. Bells started ringing. The kids grew interested and wanted to hear more.

Other times, you will find a broken home where kids need friendship and activity. Your church can provide that. Be a church that meets needs and you will reach a lot of needy people.

5. *Present the Gospel when you have earned the family's trust.*

There is a great debate possible here, but I hope you will hear me out. God's plan of salvation is certainly simple, but it represents a major change from the lifestyles of our generation. Many people have been saved in other days whose salvation decision followed years of hearing but not understanding the Gospel. Soulwinners visited the home, took a walk down that famous Romans Road, and a new Christian was born. It all looked so simple. But after investigation you will find that much seed had been sown by others in earlier days. This was the day to reap the harvest.

As our culture becomes more secular you will find that most genuine decisions for Christ will not come that easily. To accept Christ is to make the major decision of a lifetime. While the Holy Spirit of God can powerfully and quickly break through walls of sin and unbelief, this work is sometimes a process rather than a one-time event.

Our culture was once built on the principles of God's Word. Common ground already existed as you began to talk with people about their need of Christ. This is a different day.

You need to build relationships with people before they will be ready to hear your message. When the time is right, make your presentation and make it clear!

But when is the time right? You will need to be the judge of that. Craig and Troy were recruited by the bus captain, came to church, and both received the Lord. Then they returned to the mobile home park to tell their Catholic parents all about it.

Dave and Marlene were good, decent people. But they were not quite sure what all of this was about. So the next Sunday they rode the bus themselves to find out what was going on. They had seen the change in their sons, had heard a little about what had happened at church, and now they were ready to learn more. Soon they, too, trusted Christ as Savior. Dave decided to quit his job, go in business for himself, and enroll in the church's Bible institute. This fine couple now faithfully directs the junior department at an inner-city ministry. Their lives are great testimonies for the saving power of Christ, and it all began with their children.

Once the family (or any part of it) has trusted the Lord, the next important part of your work begins. One of the greatest oversights of many modern churches is the failure to disciple new believers. This spiritual child neglect often results in people trusting Christ, perhaps following the Lord in baptism, then six months later evaporating from the church completely. Evangelism without discipleship is like giving birth to a baby and then leaving the child in a box at the neighbor's front door. Be sure the workers from the adult ministry quickly begin discipleship if you cannot do it yourself.

6. *Always end your visit with prayer.*

Taking the needs of this family before the Lord is a sure way to begin the process of helping people where they are. You will be more likely to remember to pray in the future if you begin with the people before you. Families will be blessed as you lay your hand on their child's shoulder praying that this young life might grow to honor Christ.

Ask the family about special needs you can remember in your prayers as you leave. Families are often quick to discern when someone really cares, and they will be grateful that the Lord sent you along. You will sometimes learn that people are in the middle of a crisis, or about to face great challenges that call for the help of God's people.

7. *Keep a record of your visits.*

Write down the results of your visits for further reference. Once several teens and I took over a dying Sunday School bus route. At the center of the route was an apartment project of 180 low-rent units. I bought a small spiral-bound notebook I could keep in my pocket out of view. Then I set aside one page for each apartment, posting the apartment number at the top of the page. Finally, we went to work.

I entered on my page everything I could learn about the family. I noted times they were not at home to see if I could draw conclusions about the family schedule. I jotted down names of children and dogs, whether this was a one or two-parent family, church affiliation, and whether their response was friendly or otherwise. If the response was negative but I felt I should follow up with another visit, I noted this and listed whether the visit should come in a week, a month or in six months. We visited each apartment twice a year in case new people had moved in since our last visit.

The results were astounding. I became known as the pastor of the apartment project. We reached many kids and several complete families in that complex of families. And many other people who never visited our church were blessed nonetheless by our prayers, our encouragement, and our love.

You will soon find that traditional visitation yields to relationships and times spent together as the family of God. Remember you never get a second chance to make a good first impression. Plan carefully what you want to happen, and go in the power of God!

Chapter Five

REVIEW QUESTIONS:

1. List seven basic principles for a successful visit.

2. What are eight possible reasons for visiting a child's home?

3. Why should you end every visit in prayer?

DISCUSSION QUESTIONS:

1. What common mistakes do church workers make in visitation? How can they be avoided?

2. Should men always go in coats and ties and ladies go in skirts or dresses when making visits? How does our dress affect the reception we receive? Should we ever "dress down" to a more casual style that would be comfortable to the people we are visiting?

3. What are the potential hazards of visiting alone?

Chapter Six

TEACHING THE BIBLE TO CHILDREN

Chapter Six

TEACHING THE BIBLE TO CHILDREN

I went to church every Sunday for over six years when I was a child. (I do not like the term "go to church" because the church is an organism of God's people. To say "go to church" is like saying "go to family." You don't go to family, you are a part of the family. But realizing that so many people use the term in this loose way, we will save that discussion for another time.)

Whatever you want to call it, I was there each Lord's Day. The general assembly was first, followed by the Sunday morning service. (They did not have a children's church, so I sat in the front row under the watchful eye of my mother in the choir.) Sunday night we came back for whatever it was they had. And we came on Wednesday night every now and then, too.

After all these hours of biblical instruction I should have known my stuff; but I vaguely knew only a few of the stories. I did not understand the main message of the Bible, and none of the other kids in my classes seemed to know much more.

Growing up and becoming a teacher of children, I quickly realized that my teaching needed to be more effective than the instruction I had received as a child. Through trial and error and lots of study I came to develop a style that effectively communicated to boys and girls. Each time I stand before a group of kids I learn a little more about the teaching-learning process and how I can do a better job. But some principles of teaching have become clear. I call them the "Ten Commandments for teachers." Let's look at them together now.

The Ten Commandments for Teachers
1. Teach the entire Bible.

There are 40 or so Bible stories that every teacher knows and loves to tell. A good exercise would be to stop now and list your favorites.

These are certainly important. Children need to hear their messages. However, the Bible is filled with people, events, and blessings from God that we often miss because of our own lack of Bible knowledge. Here is a list of my favorite forgotten heroes that you may never have met.

Have you met...

- *Ittai the Gittite?* His loyalty to a leader contains a lesson for us all. You will find him in 2 Samuel 15:19.

- *The Rechabites?* Their obedience to the command of an ancestor saved their lives several times and allowed them to be used by God as an obedience illustration of obedience to the nation.

- *Jahaziel?* 2 Chronicles chapter 20 records the story. Although he never wrote a book of the Bible, this prophet was used mightily by God to deliver a message of assurance to strengthen the faith of the people at the hour of their greatest need.

- *Barnabas?* Although many have heard of this mighty man, few know that he was the man who discipled the apostle Paul and provided the encouragement to help Paul grow to become the greatest missionary of all time.

A *curriculum* is a planned program of study. You do not teach the curriculum. You teach the Bible according to the plan of the curriculum. A good one will help you teach the entire Bible on the level of the hearers.

Perhaps your involvement with curriculum planning is slight. If you are a Sunday School teacher you probably receive the quarterly teacher's edition and a stack of pupil books. There you will typically find thirteen lessons, broken into three units of study and all built around a basic Bible theme.

But let's consider another idea. Suppose you cannot find a curriculum you really enjoy. Or suppose it is your responsibility to plan a Sunday evening program. There are many good curriculum resources in the average Christian bookstore. One common weakness is an emphasis on the application of Scriptural truth without providing enough Scriptural truth to really apply. What would you do if you could formulate your own plan of study? You know the children need a good foundation of biblical knowledge, carefully applied to their lives. You want to teach them the Book. But how should you teach it?

Teach the Bible chronologically

Younger children can be taught a quarter of Old Testament followed by a quarter from the New. But juniors can be taught to see the entire picture...to follow the story of the Bible in the order that it happened. We created a Junior Bible Institute program at my former church, that took the children through the entire Bible in 52 weeks. Each year we emphasized different truths. The study was short enough that they could stand back and visualize the entire story, but long enough that we could present many important truths. Here is a suggestion as to what you might teach each week to cover the entire Bible in a year.

\multicolumn{2}{c}{**Teaching the Bible Chronologically**}	
Week 1	Introduction: What is the Bible? Why do we study it? What is inspiration?
2	The creation of all things; why God made the earth and all that is in it
3	The fall of man and God's provision to cover his sin
4	The flood and the tower of Babel; man's rebellion against God
5	The call of Abraham; the place of the Jews in God's plan
6	The faith of Abraham; the offering of Isaac; how was Abraham saved?
7	Jacob and Essau; understanding eternal values
8	The life of Joseph; Joseph's obedience, rise to power, and forgiving spirit
9	The Jews in slavery and the call of Moses
10	The Passover; looking to the cross of Christ
11	The Exodus; the Jews' unbelief in spite of God's faithfulness
12	Mt. Sinai: the Commandments; why God gave the law
13	The tabernacle and the priesthood
14	The unbelief at Kadesh-Barnea and the wilderness wanderings
15	The final words and death of Moses; the call of Joshua
16	The conquest and the fall of Jericho
17	The sin at Ai; the deceit of the Gibeonites
18	The later days of Joshua; the testimony of Caleb; Joshua's 3 choices
19	The period of the Judges and the life of Ruth
20	The childhood and ministry of Samuel
21	Israel wants a king: the rise and fall of Saul
22	The Psalms
23	The life of David: his faith, his sin, and his boldness before God
24	The book of Proverbs; understanding godly wisdom

25	The rise and fall of Solomon
26	The foolishness of Rehoboam and the divided kingdom
27	The kings of Israel; the captivity of the northern kingdom
28	The prophets: their life and work; the messages they proclaimed
29	The kings of Judah: the royal line of David
30	The fall of Jerusalem and the Babylonian captivity
31	The godly men of the book of Daniel
32	The book of Esther: how God can use me if I am available
33	The return and rebuilding of the temple
34	Nehemiah and the walls of Jerusalem
35	The prophets after the return
36	The prophecies and birth of Christ
37	The ministry of John the Baptist; the baptism and temptation of Christ
38	The parables of Christ: why he told them and what he taught
39	What we learn about Christ through his miracles
40	The gospel of John: understanding who Jesus really is
41	The commands of Christ: what are we to do?
42	The last week of Christ's life
43	The resurrection and ascension of Christ
44	The Great Commission and the day of Pentecost; the early church
45	The persecutions and spreading of the Gospel
46	The conversion and early days of the apostle Paul
47	The missionary journeys of Paul
48	The book of Romans: understanding salvation
49	The other letters of Paul
50	The books of Hebrews and James; help for Christian Jews
51	False teachings in the early church
52	The revelation of Jesus Christ to John

Teach the Bible doctrinally

The important "doctrines" (teachings) of the Bible make up the foundation of our faith. We must know what we believe and why, not just that we believe. Bible doctrines are often thought of as dry studies of the finer points of scriptural truth. But for the Christian, the doctrines of the Bible make up the basis for our lives before the Lord. God's commands are always based upon basic scriptural truths. We are told to be holy because God is holy. We are told to be faithful because Christ is coming back to take us home. The final three chapters of the book of Ephesians show us how to live, but they follow the first three chapters that explain our relationship to Christ.

Children can and must be taught Bible doctrine. Later in this chapter we will provide suggestions that will show you how to teach these truths. Let's talk about what we should teach and the doctrines that constitute our curriculum. Here is a year's supply of questions you should answer.

Teaching the Bible Doctrinally	
DOCTRINE	**QUESTION**
The Trinity	1. How do we know there is a God?
	2. What is God like?
God the Father	3. What has God ever done for me?
Jesus Christ	4. Is Jesus God, too? How do we know? How could He be God and human at the same time?
	5. What was Jesus doing before He came to earth as a baby?
	6. What do the names of Jesus mean?
	7. Why do we say Jesus is a prophet, a priest, and a king?
	8. Why did Jesus die on the cross?

The Resurrection	9. How do we know for sure that Jesus rose again from the dead? Why is it important?
The Holy Spirit	10. Is the Spirit of God a he or an it? What does He do?
	11. What did the Holy Spirit do to make me a Christian?
	12. What has the Holy Spirit given me? How does He help me today?
Man	13. Why did God make us?
	14. How did sin come into the world?
	15. What is a person like who has never become a Christian?
	16. What changes take place when I become a child of God?
Hell	17. What is hell like? How could a loving God send people there?
Heaven	18. What is heaven like? How can I go there?
The Church	19. What is a church?
	20. What are baptism and the Lord's Supper all about?
	21. What do pastors and deacons do?
	22. What is my role in the church?
Sin	23. What is sin? Where did it come from?
	24. How did Jesus pay for my sin?
	25. What should I do when I am tempted?
Salvation	26. What is salvation?
	27. How did Old Testament truths prepare God's people to understand salvation?
	28. Why do we need to be reconciled to God?
	29. What is repentance?
	30. How did Christ redeem me?
	31. What does it mean to be born again?
	32. What is imputation all about?
	33. What is justification?

Salvation (cont.)	34. What does it mean to be holy?
	35. What will I be like in heaven? What is glorification?
	36. Can I ever lose my salvation?
	37. What are the three aspects (past, present, and future) of my salvation?
	38. Does God want everyone saved?
	39. Why did God save me?
	40. How can I know for sure that I am saved?
Satan	41. Why did God create Satan? What is he like? What does he do?
Angels	42. Why did God make angels? Are there bad angels? What do angels do?
The Bible	43. How was the Bible written? What is inspiration?
	44. How has the Bible been passed down to us?
	45. Did God really give the Bible to tell us what is true and to show us how to live?
	46. Are there mistakes in the Bible? Is every word true?
Prophecy	47. What prophecies of the future have already been fulfilled?
	48. Is Jesus really coming back? When is He coming? Why is He coming?
	49. What will happen during the Tribulation?
	50. What is the Millennium? What will it be like?
	51. How will the world be judged?
	52. What will eternity be like? How can I be ready?

Teach the Bible practically

Children need to know the "how to's" of the Bible. These are the basic skills of Christianity, the daily lifestyle of the believer. Also included are the basic struggles and opportunities believers face and how the Christian child should respond to them. Here is a full year of questions you might answer in your Bible studies.

Teaching the Bible Practically	
TOPIC OF DISCUSSION	**QUESTIONS TO BE ANSWERED**
Assurance	1. How can I know for sure that I am a Christian? 2. What does it mean when God forgives me?
Identifying with Christ	3. What is baptism? 4. How should I let others know I am a Christian?
Relationships	5. How can I learn to get along?
Friendship	6. How can I be a good friend? 7. My best friend stole something of mine. What should I do?
Prayer	8. What is prayer? How can I get what I need from God?
Praise	9. How can I praise God?
Worship	10. How can I worship God?
The Christian in the World	11. Why did Jesus call us "the light of the world"? 12. How can I share my faith with others? 13. Should I have friends who are not Christians?
Persecution	14. Why do the kids at school laugh at me when I take my Bible along? What should I do? How should I respond?

Money	15. How can I use my money to please the Lord? How should I give to God?
Honoring God with my words	16. What does God teach about the words I say?
	17. What words should I not say?
	18. How can I speak encouraging words to others?
Missions	19. What is a missionary?
	20. How will I know if God wants me to become one?
Serving God	21. How can God use me every day?
	22. Do kids have spiritual gifts, too?
	23. How can I become a responsible servant?
Heroes	24. Who are the proper role models for me?
	25. Suppose my favorite athlete is not a Christian? Should I hang his poster in my room?
Right and wrong	26. Is it ever right to do wrong?
	27. Is it ever right to lie?
	28. How can I decide what is right if the Bible is not clear?
Temptation	29. How can I say "no" when Satan says "yes"?
Time with God	30. How can I have an effective quiet time?
Suffering	31. Why do bad things happen to good people?
Authority	32. Why has God placed authorities over me?
	33. Who are these authorities? What do they do?
	34. What is obedience? What is rebellion?
	35. What should I do if an authority asks me to do something wrong?
	36. Should I obey bad laws?
Current issues	37. Does the Bible talk about AIDS?
	38. What is abortion? Why is it wrong?
	39. Is war wrong? Why is there so much fighting?

Peer pressure	40. How can I live like a Christian at school?
	41. What can I do when my friends do wrong?
	42. How can I stand alone?
The fruit of the spirit	43. How does God want to change my life?
Moral purity	44. How can I keep a clean mind in a dirty world?
Prejudice	45. Why are others not like me?
Wisdom	46. What is godly wisdom?
	47. How can I be wise?
Anger	48. Is it ever right to be mad?
	49. What can I do about a bad temper?
	50. Suppose I am bitter about something someone did? What should I do?
Sin	51. What should I do if I did wrong?
	52. How can I obey God when it is really hard?

Perhaps you say, "These are very interesting questions? But where do I find the answers?" I have two responses to your question. The first will take you to your local bookstore where you will find hundreds of books, Bible study courses, and other materials to help. Perhaps you could label a file folder for each question, and file away materials as you find them. You may need to take one lesson from this resource and another lesson from that book. Or perhaps you will find one source that answers many of these questions. Even Bible study materials for teens or adults can be adapted for your needs. You will find more suggestions in a special section in the back of this book.

Another place to find answers is directly from the Bible itself. As you work with children and spend time with them, you will begin to understand their culture, their thinking processes, and the problems they face. Then as you spend time studying the Bible you will grow in your understanding of how God thinks and the resources He has made available to all of us. Little by little your ideas will grow as you create your own unique ways of communicating these truths to your children.

You could take the 156 previously mentioned lesson suggestions and produce a one-year curriculum; teach the Bible chronologically on Sunday morning, practically on Sunday evening, and doctrinally at the mid-week service. Or create a three-year Sunday School curriculum. The same scriptural truths you will find in teaching the Bible one way will also appear while using another method of study. The review will help seal these vital truths in the minds of your students.

Never forget how much Bible you can teach if you will use the time you have. Do not spend too much time with sword drills, games, and trips to the playground. Use every second (realizing that sometimes you will teach with drills and games) to accomplish your goals for the morning. But what are those goals?

2.   Have a lesson aim.

Each time you stand before your class you should fully understand what you want to accomplish while you are there. We have already learned that we want our children to become more like Christ. But that is too general a statement to explain the purpose of one lesson. We want to teach the children the entire Bible, but not the entire Book every time we meet! So what small part of our total job do we want to accomplish during the next hour of Sunday School, during my Junior Church lesson or during devotions tonight at camp?

The teacher's responsiblity is to formulate a lesson aim. This statement of purpose provides a short, measurable goal that will be a guide in deciding what to teach and how to teach it. A good lesson aim has three distinctive characteristics.

A good lesson aim is...
1. *Clear* enough to be written down
2. *Short* enough to be remembered
3. *Specific* enough to be achieved

Making it clear – If you cannot jot down your lesson aim, it is probably not very clear in your mind. The experts tell us that when visiting the grocery store it is best to take along a shopping list. You will be sure to bring home what you need and may even be protected from the temptation to buy everything in the store that looks good!

A lesson aim is like a shopping list. It tells you why you are there and what you want to happen before you leave. It is a "things to do today" list to help you determine that this lesson will not be wasted. You will resist the temptation to wander from the topic at hand to whatever crosses your mind. (Sometimes, however, it is quite acceptable to go into unplanned territory; the questions asked by your students will often point out needs that must be met today.)

Making it short – Any lesson aim that can be accomplished within one class period is going to be short enough that you can memorize it before you begin. If your lesson aim grows too long, you are probably setting out to do too much.

Making it specific – When you visit the drive-thru at the fast-food restaurant you don't just ask for food. You tell them that you want three large burgers, two small fries, one medium diet Coke, one medium unsweetened tea, and a milk.

Your lesson aim should be just that specific. Just saying you want to teach about prayer is not enough. You need to answer some questions before you fully understand why you are not over in the main auditorium

with the rest of the grown-ups instead of standing before these kids!

• What specifically do you want the students to learn
  about the topic?

• What change do you want to see in their attitudes
  and feelings?

• What exactly are the students to do about what you
  will teach? What is the expected response?

I like to think of these questions in terms of "know,
show, and grow" aims! Here is an example. This could
be the lesson aim (aims) of a 6th-grade lesson on the
subject of peer pressure. The text is Daniel chapter 1.
Our lesson will deal with Daniel's response to the command that they eat the food and drink the beverage
from the king's table, a meal that would cause them to
disobey God.

My students should KNOW:

• the pressures Daniel faced and how they are similar to our own struggles.

• how Daniel responded to these pressures.

• the result of Daniel's obedience.

My students should SHOW:

• a desire to obey God in the face of pressure to do
  what others do.

• a willingness to stand alone.

My students should GROW:

• by listing typical pressures they face.

• by applying the principles Daniel followed when
  faced with pressure from his peers.

If a lesson aim is not included in your curriculum (or if you are writing your own), define your lesson aims before you begin your final study. If an aim is provided, study it carefully and see if you can refine it to better meet the needs of your class. In short, never go to class unless you fully understand why you are there. And after each class, evaluate what you have accomplished to see if you met your aims. The final standard by which you should measure success is what happens in the lives of your students. These results may begin today, but they will continue a lifetime!

3. Understand the limitations and abilities of your students.

What kind of teacher was Jesus? He was simply the best there is. None was ever better. But what made Him the best? What did He do that we can do too? Most of us have heard unflattering reviews of some of our lessons. What did the people say about His?

The Bible tells us in Mark 1:22 that "the people were amazed at his teaching, because he taught like a person who had authority, not like their teachers of the law." The people were shocked because this teacher knew how to teach. He talked like He knew what He was talking about!

You can be a teacher like that. Part of the process is to understand those students sitting before you and know what you must do to communicate to their minds, their hearts, and their lives.

Age is a factor

As a student matures, his ability to learn matures as well. Many changes take place in the learning process as a child grows older.

• *Vocabulary* – The words you use must be appropriate

for the age level of the children. Younger children need simple words of few syllables. Listen to Mr. Rogers on TV. He knows his audience well!

• *Attention span* – Have you ever watched Sesame Street on television? Each program consists of over twenty short little episodes that work together to accomplish the goals of the day. (Lesson aim: "Sesame Street was brought to you today by the letters F and P and the number 9.") The intended viewers all possess a short little attention span, and no segment takes longer than a child can comprehend. It is generally understood that a child's attention span is sixty to ninety seconds for every year of his age. That doesn't mean your lesson cannot last any longer than that. You, like Bert and Ernie, can break your lesson into different activities and experiences that all work together to accomplish your lesson aim for today.

• *Ability to comprehend* – Kindergarten children think differently than fifth graders do. While younger children think very concretely, older children can understand symbolic truth ("I am the bread of life") and apply principles to general situations. Also, remember that we learn by building upon past experiences. Jesus used illustrations of sheep, farmers and their crops, and fishing because that was what the people knew. The better you understand your children and their culture, the better your illustrations will hit home. The world of the five-year-old is built around a secure school class, home, and parents. Older children have broadened their experiences through friends, television, and reading. Be sure you speak to those children who sit before you.

Consider the culture of your students

Are your children from the country, the suburbs or the city? Their zip codes will make a difference in the way you teach. I once pastored a large group of children that included Christian school kids, children of Bible professors, boys and girls from blue collar homes, and inner-city children from single-parent homes. We quickly divided the kids into classes by culture. It wasn't that the white shirt and ties crowd did not want to sit next to the tee shirt and jeans; these kids spoke different cultural languages although they all lived within a ten-minute drive of the others' homes! We found we could best minister to them if we divided them into groups with similar cultural environments.

To tell a child that God is like a father will mean one thing to my son; it will mean something else entirely to the child of a drunk who beats him and his mother.

Be aware of physical limitations

Billy wiggled a lot; that was okay. But he could never remember anything. He wouldn't bring his Bible, he did not complete his worksheet, and he never had anything to add to the discussion. What was wrong with this little guy? What did we need to deal with here?

Billy had learning disabilities that affected everything he did. Once we knew that, we understood how to interpret his actions. Your class will include a wide range of intelligence and ability levels. Be discreet and gentle with your expectations.

4. Use lots of illustrations.

Jesus did that, and the people understood. We are told He never taught without lots of stories that would make his message clear (Matt. 13:34). This does not mean that as he taught he would smile and say, "that reminds me of a story." His illustrations were specifically chosen and carefully designed to make his point clearer. Stories were never told for their own sake alone.

What kind of illustrations can you use? Let's look at some verbal ones.

- *Stories* – Children are quick to remember simple stories that express simple truths. The kids at my church know how wrong I was to sneak on that bus without paying when I was a child. They all remember how God saved my life when I obeyed my mother's instructions to put on my life jacket ten minutes before the boat tipped over. And they will never forget how my dog followed the school bus and entered my first-grade class, just as we are to be followers of Jesus Christ. You can even make up stories like Jesus did (if you carefully explain to the kids that this is a "let's suppose" story.)

- *Examples* – You will find great examples in the newspaper and on television every day. While watching the Olympics on television I saw a touching sight. The face of a runner suddenly froze as pain shot through his leg. He was no longer a serious contender and could hardly walk. But then something wonderful happened! A man rushed from the stands, held the runner with his arms, and helped the weakened athlete across the finish line. The man who helped was the runner's father! And our heavenly father is just like that! But would Jesus use illustrations from the events of his day? Read Luke 13:4 for a fine example. We do not know anything else about that tower in Siloam or the eighteen who died, but the crowd who heard Jesus that day knew all about it.

- *Testimonies* – Personally sharing how the truth being taught was internalized into your life is quite effective. Ask adults or children to give testimonies. Once I taught a series of lessons that challenged the boys and girls to stand alone for God, especially in school. Each Sunday morning one of the kids shared a situation from the preceding week that affirmed the blessings of standing for Christ.

5. Arouse curiosity.

One of the greatest tools available to the teacher is the natural curiosity in every boy and girl. If you teach with an overhead projector, only reveal one point at a time. Vary your teaching methods. Never let your students know what you are going to do next.

Lance was a great kid, but he spent most Sunday mornings at the back of the auditorium. He was growing in the Lord and certainly wasn't against what was going on up front, but the social center of any Junior Church tends to be toward the back of the room. That is where he spent his time. Until one Sunday morning.

I wanted to teach a lesson on yielding our rights to God. All the kids knew about Judge Wampner and the "People's Court", so I set the room up to copy the set of the popular show. There was a bench up front (with a small nameplate identifying me as the judge, "The Honorable Herbert T. Dumpster"). The "People's Court" sign was large and graced the side wall. There was a stand for the defendant and another for the plaintiff. When I majestically came in on the front row, there sat Lance *on the front row.*

I whispered the inevitable question, "What are you doing up here?"

"Oh," he replied, "I didn't want to miss anything!"

I never forgot the lesson Lance taught me that day. "Let 'em wonder what you're going to do!"

I do not remember who first taught me this amazing truth, but it has proved itself over and over as I have taught boys and girls.

> **A child, generally speaking, will do the first thing that comes to his mind. Therefore, to control the child, you must control his mind.**

If the kids are not paying attention to the lesson, it is because you are not the most exciting show in the room. You will want to plan something interesting that will arouse the children's curiosity at frequent intervals throughout the lesson.

6.   Use humor and drama to communicate.

Your class does not need the services of a stand-up comic, but you will find that occasional humor will help keep interest strong and win the loyalty of your children. Older children respond well to subtle humor and puns; younger kids go wild over slapstick. Find your own style of humor, do not overuse it, and know where it fits in the lesson.

Our children love to hear all of the stupid things that I have done that illustrate the point at hand. A good teacher will learn to tell a story in such a way that the kids are on the edge of their seats, waiting for the conclusion. If you are going to teach you will need to polish your verbal skills so you can communicate the truth to the children.

Let's pretend: you own a growing corporation that sells products to retail establishments. The Acme Widget Company has several departments that relate to the way you teach your lesson.

Research and development parallel your study as you get the product ready for market. What does the Bible say? What are we to do about it? What are the people's needs?

Marketing is very important; a good widget will sit on the shelf until someone wants to buy. Who might buy my product? What should the box look like? The name of the product, the way it is packaged, and the way it is presented to the buyer all have a part in its eventual success or failure. Having a good lesson is not enough. It must be taught in such a way that the students' attention is captured and the truth is presented in a clear, interesting way. Package the truth in a form that the children will want to receive and understand.

7. Be visual.

Your students have five senses. The more of those senses you keep busy, the better job you will do of sealing the lesson in their lives. Never teach a lesson with words alone. Use visual aids, props, and demonstrations to help you on your way.

Be sure to change the kind of visual aids you use from time to time. Flannelgraph is great, but not every week! Use slides, transparencies, charts, and teaching pictures. Use real objects when possible. But to really make your lessons visual there is something more you can do.

Alan was an unusual guy. He helped me with the juniors while he was in college and excelled as a Bible teacher. His vocal skills were average. He had a quiet personality, but he could wonderfully visualize biblical truth!

To teach the Old Testament he turned our Wednesday evening program into a news broadcast. We had sets, slides, and news reports from around the biblical world. He also created a weekly newspaper of the events as they appeared in our Bible studies. What a program! What a teacher!

One summer at camp his Bible students experienced the book of Revelation in a most unusual way. He invited me in for the marriage supper of the lamb. The table was set in fine tableware (plastic, but it looked like the real thing) with goblets of grape juice and linen-white tablecloths. To enter the room, the students passed through the door of eternal life. A throne was even set at the end of the table for the King Himself!

One father told me, "My son loved camp; but he will never forget the book of Revelation!"

Do you remember the story of Elijah and the prophets of Baal? That bull was but a large visual aid to help the people understand the weakness of Baal and the strength of Jehovah. The tabernacle was an even larger visual aid to help the people understand Jesus Christ. Once, when teaching about the feeding of the 5,000, we distributed small fish stick pieces and little biscuits to help the children remember.

Then there was the time Joe Brown called about the cake. He ran a bakery and a customer had ordered a large wedding cake but never came to pick it up. (I always wondered why, but let's get back to my story.) He asked if I could use it, and I told him that in fact I did know a couple hundred kids who might like a slice. My wheels began to turn. Soon, I had a plan.

I made a few calls (in fact, *quite* a few) and finally found a mom of one of the kids in the church who not only still had her wedding dress but would still fit in it. The next morning her husband wore his good suit, she wore the wedding gown, and their son gave away the bride as I remarried the couple and taught the kids about Christian marriage. And, of course, a reception followed in the church fellowship hall – cake and all!

How would you teach about death and what follows? We borrowed a casket from the local funeral home. After the funeral the body opened the lid, got out, and stood before the throne. The kids never forgot that one either!

8. Fully involve your students in the lesson.

Kids have a hard time sitting still for very long and not squirming. So get them involved and let them be a part. When teaching younger children about the healing of Bartimaeus you will quickly discover they do not fully understand what blindness really is. Play games where the children are blindfolded to begin the lesson. One of our teachers helped the children make pipe cleaner glasses and walk around looking at brightly-colored posters to help them appreciate their eyesight.

Develop a collection of biblical costumes and plan act-it-out plays where the children relive the stories. Your children could pretend that they are the characters in the story (even without costumes). Ask them what they would do, how they would feel, and what problems they would face. Or put your children into modern situations, giving them problems and asking for solutions.

How would you teach the Passover? I found a way that captures the attention of the children, gets them totally involved, and teaches a lesson they will never forget. But it takes a little time. Cover the area in front of the room with a plastic drop cloth or newspaper. Set up a folding table on your floor covering, and decorate it to look like an altar. Have a large butcher knife ready and in plain view.

Teach the children about the slavery in Egypt, the discouragement of the Jews, and God's plan for deliverance. Explain the purpose of the lamb, how the blood would be shed, and the Passover promise. Build the whole thing up with a flourish to be sure the children understand what would happen to that poor animal. And then you dramatically bring in a beautiful young lamb. Place the lamb on the altar, raise the knife, and be assured that you will have the attention of every child in the room!

At that point, share the good news that you do not need to kill that lamb. Jesus shed his blood as the final sacrifice for sin. We are now free! And be assured that *the lamb* and *the Lamb* will both receive a standing ovation!

Years after I have taught that lesson parents have told me that their children would always remember it. I have never seen faces of children who understood more clearly the sacrifice of the innocent son of God!

You may not have a lamb to bring in (although I would seriously consider finding one!), but you can involve the children in such a way to make sure you have taught and they have learned.

9.   Constantly review and build on the truths your students have learned.

Perhaps you have heard of the family who took the budget USA vacation – thirty-two states in twenty-one days. Whenever they found something interesting the father would hand the kids the camera and shout, "Quick, we're in a hurry. Take a picture; you can look it when you get home!"

Sometimes we try to teach the Bible that way. We need to "get through the material" so fast that none of it becomes a part of us or the children. Never try to teach too much, and be sure to constantly review, apply, and build on what was learned in the past.

The best Bible teacher I ever heard was a wiry little guy, but was also amazing. He would come to the university from time to time. The student body loved every minute at his feet, learning the Word of God. I remember some of his outlines and many of his illustrations, but I will never forget how he would end every message. He'd say, "Next time we'll begin with two minutes of quick review, then on we go!" Perhaps that was the most important thing he ever taught me: begin each new lesson with a look back to where we have already been before.

By referring to the rebellion of the Jews as they stood before the Red Sea we understand more God's disgust at Kadesh-Barnea. Luke begins the book of Acts by reviewing what he wrote in his gospel, already received by Theophilus. Paul often reviewed Old Testament truth to make New Testament application. God even wrote a little song and taught it to Moses, who would then teach it to the Jews. The song would review their past rebellions against God so they would understand His present judgment.

If the Jews had trouble remembering what God had taught them, you can be sure your own students will be equally prone to forget. So make your teaching like building blocks; lay principle upon principle, truth upon truth, and doctrine upon doctrine.

One way is to begin each lesson with activities, worksheets, and games that review the lessons of the previous weeks. Or give assignments based on what was learned. The students can report back the next week and share how the truth was applied.

10.   Teach with God's help.

The best prepared lesson will be a flop without the touch of God. Pray each step along the way of preparation, teaching, and application that God would use your work for His glory.

Begin with early preparation. If you are a Sunday School teacher you should look over the quarterly before you teach the first lesson to grasp the direction your teaching will take. As you begin each unit you will look ahead to see where each lesson will take you. And begin the final preparation for each lesson as soon as the previous lesson has been taught. Ask yourself some hard questions that will show you how well you did. Begin your study early in the week, carefully thinking through what you want to say and how you want to say it. Think of illustrations that will be appropriate and plan how you will visualize your lesson. Ask God's help in every step of the process. You do not know what will be on the heart of your students when they arrive, but God most certainly does. Our work is of no avail if it does not produce eternal results.

Chapter Six

REVIEW QUESTIONS:

1. List the ten commandments for teachers.

2. From what three perspectives can you teach the Bible to children?

3. What are the characteristics of a lesson aim?

DISCUSSION QUESTIONS:

1. Are there some parts of the Bible that should not be taught to younger children? Are longer studies through complete books of the Bible ever appropriate for children? Should "family values education" that deals with topics such as sexual morality be taught to children?

2. How do we teach the Bible in classes with larger age spans? If we must include grades one through six in Junior Church, how do we teach to meet the needs of all?

3. What are some other ways of involving the children in the teaching-learning process? Do plays, discussions, and Bible learning games take time away from teaching Bible content? At what point does our teaching emphasize too much application and too little content?

Chapter Seven

LEADING A CHILD
TO CHRIST

Chapter Seven

LEADING A CHILD TO CHRIST

The most eternal thing you will ever do is to lead a child to saving faith in Jesus Christ. But what about the little boy who comes forward at every invitation? And what should we think about kids who make professions but soon thereafter drop out of church? What can we do to help children make genuine decisions? How can we be sure we are doing the right thing?

These questions are not easily answered. There is no one way to be sure we adequately explain the Gospel and gently lead children to faith in Christ. But we want to do the best we can. In this chapter we will make some specific suggestions you should consider when helping children understand and respond to the call of God.

1. Be certain you clearly understand what salvation really is.

Many fine children's workers have felt inadequate in helping children come to Christ. The first step toward success is to clearly understand salvation yourself.

Our problem: sin.

Throughout Scripture God paints a sad picture of the true nature of the people he has created. King Solomon reminded the Lord:

"There is no man that sinneth not" (1 Kings 8:46).

Isaiah lamented at our rebellion against God.

"All we like sheep have gone astray; we have turned every one to his own way" (Isa. 53:6).

The prophet Jeremiah explained the reason for our rebellion.

"The heart is deceitful above all things, and desperately wicked: who can know it" (Jer. 17:9).

And the apostle John warned:

"If we say that we have no sin, we deceive ourselves, and the truth is not in us" (1 John 1:8).

The results of our problem: separation from God.

Many people fail to fully understand the results of their sin. Many people simply think of an eternity in hell; but it is far worse than that. We are separated from God now! Isaiah explained it clearly.

"But your iniquities (sins) have separated between you and your God, and your sins have hid his face from you, that he will not hear" (Isa. 59:2).

We are not sinners because we sin; we sin because we were born sinners! (See Psalm 51:5 and Romans 5:12.) We came into this world with a sinful nature that leads us into sin. We are born separated from God.

God's desire: that we might be at peace with Him.

Picture in your mind a nighttime scene during the Civil War. On one side of the river camped the Army of the United States, while on the other waited the Army of Northern Virginia. The people of America had been divided by strife; and the only way peace would come would be for one side to surrender, fully agreeing to terms laid down by the victor.

That well describes the relationship between mankind and God. We are born at war with Him. The goal of God is that the two parties might be reconciled so that the war might be over. The apostle Paul understood this. Not only was he grateful that he had made peace with God; he recognized his duty to help others be reconciled as well.

"And all things are of God, who hath reconciled us to himself by Jesus Christ, and hath given to us the ministry of reconciliation" (2 Cor. 5:18).

Christ's death: our way back to God.

Our lives were being destroyed by sin: our sinful nature and our wrong choices. Yet Christ lived on earth, facing the same temptations we face each day, but He never sinned. So when Christ died, it became possible for our sins to be placed on Him. He was punished for our wrongs. God then took his perfect nature (we call it "righteousness") and gave it to us. He took what we had so that we can take what He has that we need so desperately.

"For he hath made him to be sin for us, who knew no sin; that we might be made the righteousness of God in him" (2 Cor. 5:21).

All of those "he's" and "him's" may be a little hard to follow. Let's check the New Century Version for a clearer explanation.

"Christ has no sin, but God made him become sin so that in Christ we could become right with God" (2 Cor. 5:21 NCV).

The missing ingredient: faith.

It is our faith in what Jesus did on the Cross and in His resurrection from the dead that makes salvation ours. Paul explains it clearly.

"For by grace are you saved through faith; and that not of yourselves: it is the gift of God: Not of works, lest any man should boast" (Eph. 2:8-9).

God gave us the desire and the power to trust Christ as Savior. It was totally a gift from Him. Nothing we have ever done helped one bit. Our good deeds, our religious acts, all of our efforts are useless in taking away our sin. Only our faith in the death and resurrection of Christ (and in all that it accomplished) makes salvation ours. We have nothing to brag about; we did not have one thing to do with it. It was God's kindness, mercy, and love that made salvation possible. Our faith in what Christ did makes us at peace with God. The hymn writer explained it clearly:

In my hand no price I bring,
Simply to thy cross I cling.

2. Make your Gospel presentation a process, not a one-time event.

We have already touched upon this important point. Children learn truths that build upon other truths they already understand. This process takes time. If you are a Sunday School teacher, explain more about the Gospel each time you meet with the children. If you are a leader in Vacation Bible School, build each day's presentation on truths taught in previous days. Children seldom understand the Gospel the first time they hear it. That does not mean it never happens; but you should never assume that one presentation is enough. You may be thinking, "But the conviction comes as the Holy Spirit convinces the child of his need of Christ." But conviction is built upon understood scriptural truth (Rom. 10:14). Just as children may not understand fractions or starting up a computer the first time they try to learn, even so children may need time to fully grasp the truths of the Gospel. No one needs to master theology to come to God. But no one can be saved who does not understand the basic truths we have explained above.

You will meet many children who do not have an accurate understanding of who God really is. Our society has become confused with a myriad of false religious ideas. Many people believe it is okay to believe anything, just as long as you don't knock anyone else's beliefs!

Many who have been raised in church never clearly understood the Gospel. As a child I attended church for years, all the while assuming that coming forward, joining the church, and being baptized would take care of everything. It was not until years later that it all came into focus in my mind. Others may understand faster, but we must make certain they do understand.

3. Use accurate terms when explaining the Gospel.

I admit it: I am guilty, too. Every Sunday morning I returned home from church and listened to the choir on TV sing it so well:

If you want joy, real joy, wonderful joy,
Let Jesus come into your heart.

It sounds so nice. And many times I have urged others to let Jesus come into their hearts, too. And I meant well. But I was wrong. And we mistakenly took this idea from the Bible itself:

"Behold, I stand at the door, and knock: if any man hear my voice, and open the door, I will come in to him, and will sup with him, and he with me" (Rev. 3:20).

Don't get me wrong; the verse is true, but that door is not on our hearts. This verse is not talking about salvation. Many children have been confused as they failed to understand what we thought this verse really taught.

We also talk a lot about making a commitment and use other terms that don't mean much in themselves.

We do, most certainly, make a commitment to Christ when we become Christians. But it is more than that.

There is another mistake we can make. We sometimes use correct terms without explaining what we really mean. These terms might be part of a Christian's vocabulary, but we are talking to people who have never attended our language school. We tell them:

- Be born again.
- Be saved.
- Become a child of God.
- Become a Christian.
- Give your heart to Christ.

These are all scriptural terms. I understand these. You probably do, too. But we must be careful when talking to children (or even to older unbelievers or new Christians). We are discussing the most important truths in the world; our explanations must be clearly understood.

4. Help children visualize what you say.

We have already discussed this principle, but it is most important when presenting the Gospel. Present truths in a way that can be experienced by the children before us.

Visualizing sin.

When speaking to groups, I often bring forward the smallest little guy in the audience. I will have prepared a big suitcase so full that the young boy can hardly pick it up. I ask him to hold it while I continue to speak to the others. They don't pay much attention to me. I am being upstaged by my little helper. And that is exactly what I had in mind. He is illustrating in a clear way what it is like to carry around the burden of sin. This boy is in pain!

Visualizing Christ taking our sin.

I will call an older and bigger boy from the audience and ask him to take the suitcase. He can carry it just fine. The youngster is relieved to be rid of it. Here is where I explain how Christ took our sin and paid for it.

There is another way to explain this truth. You will need to set this one up in advance. Purchase two identical white tee shirts (or dress shirts if your crowd dresses up for church). Instruct two boys to wear the shirts to class. Ask the kids to name sins that often clutter up our lives. Then, with a felt tip pen, write these sins on one of the shirts. That will visualize our sins. Ask the two boys to go behind a curtain and exchange the shirts. Theologians call this a lesson in "imputation." Christ took our sins on the cross, and we receive his righteousness.

There are many other ways to visualize these truths. People have used chemicals, gospel magic, flannelgraph and more. Once I built a prison in class to explain how Christ paid for our sin. I released the sinner from jail and replaced him with the boy who played the part of Christ. You may think of many more ways to illustrate this.

5.   Never press a child for a decision.

I would minister and speak one way if I were at the rescue mission facing a room of alcoholics and drug pushers. But our audience today is children.

A child will often want to make a decision to please an adult, even if the child has no idea what he is deciding. Invitations in Junior Church should not consist of thirteen verses of "Just as I Am." Our methods must be gentle, carefully taken by the Holy Spirit to the human heart.

When presenting the Gospel, it is often best to ask the children to individually come to you if they would like to know more about receiving Christ. When talking with kids one on one it is also important to let the desires of the child lead the way. Explain what Christ did and what we must do. Let the child make the move when he is ready to do it.

But how young is too young? I have known five-year-olds and sometimes even younger kids who seemed to have a clear understanding of the Gospel. Their pure little hearts were without the years of sin and rebellion that often keep older people from salvation.

What about the "age of accountability"? If a child is old enough to sin and understands what he has done, he is old enough to need a Savior and to understand what he must do to come to God.

When a child is ready to receive Christ we must do our best to help him make a genuine decision. Be careful about suggesting a child "pray this prayer behind me." Salvation is not the result of prayer; it is the result of faith. When approaching Christ a child must come in complete faith: I have heard, I believe, I trust and now accept.

No book or set of instructions can provide you with just the right words for every possible situation. You must grow to fully understand the Gospel. You will need to learn how children think. You are in the delivery room where a new babe is being born. Be careful, gentle, and alert to what is taking place. You are there to do whatever you can to help new life enter the world. It is a wonderful experience.

6. Follow up decisions with discipleship.

The best way to be sure a decision was genuine is to follow it up with lots of warm Christian love, Bible teaching, and discipleship. Many times children will make decisions that are not fully understood. Further Bible teaching and instruction seals that decision and provides the assurance God has promised.

One Tuesday evening when I was sixteen I prayed the sinner's prayer after a revival service at the local church. I was in the services the next Sunday morning; present at Sunday School, worship services and later at whatever else they had. Was I born again into God's family on that Tuesday night? Or did my new birth come later as I fully understood what it was all about? I really cannot answer that. I do know now that I have been born again into God's family and I am grateful for those faithful Christians who taught me the Word of God.

Please do not misunderstand. Becoming a Christian takes place in an instant. But that instantaneous event follows a process of hearing and understanding Scriptural truth, conviction by the Holy Spirit, and faith in Christ. I have known far too many children who were pressed to "say" a prayer they did not understand and could not pray with meaning. My only warning is that we carefully present the Gospel and even more carefully lead children to express their faith in Christ.

7. Help the child remember his or her salvation experience.

One of the best ways I have found to help children remember their salvation experience is to present a "New Birth Certificate" when a child trusts Christ. The child fills it out himself and takes it home to remind himself of what has happened. It might look like this:

CERTIFICATE OF NEW BIRTH
This is to remind me that I,

John Smith

on this date

October 1, 1992

first believed that Jesus died on the cross to pay for my sin.
I also believe that He rose again from the dead and has taken
away my sin and made me a child of God.
He gave me His gift of life that will never end.
I am not a Christian because of the good things that I have
done. Today I was born, the second time, into the family of
God because He loves me. I take what He did as my own.

*For God loved the world so much that he gave his only Son.
God gave his Son so that whoever believes in him may not be
lost, but have eternal life* (John 3:16, NCV).

Signed_____

As you disciple the child you will want to have him
or her frequently verbalize his or her decision and ask
any questions he or she may have. As a child grows in
the Lord and better understands salvation, he or she
will grow in assurance and confidence in their Christian
life. Only then will you know for sure that you have, in
fact, done your best.

Chapter Seven

REVIEW QUESTIONS:

1.   What main truths make up the salvation message?

2.   What are some terms we use in presenting the Gospel that might confuse children?

3.   How can we help children visualize salvation?

DISCUSSION QUESTIONS:

1.   What are some ways we can know we are presenting truths about salvation too fast for a child to understand?

2.   Do you remember the first Gospel presentation you really understood? What made it clear? What lessons can you learn from your own experiences?

3.   What signs can we look for that tell us a child is ready to accept Christ?

Chapter Eight

SEEING THE POTENTIAL

Chapter Eight

SEEING THE POTENTIAL

I could give you a long list of reasons why I could never be a worker with children. I have never been very athletic. No one ever called me "cool." My wife and mother think I am handsome; no one else ever said so. I was shy as a child and never went to camp, never played on a team, and never had many friends. But here I am.

Maybe you have a list like mine. I have a secret. *None of our reasons make any difference.* I hope we have already shown you that God can use anyone who is willing. In this final chapter I want to help you see more clearly that you are already on your way.

I don't want to call them tricks of the trade; that might sound tacky and leave the wrong impression. But there certain attitudes that will help, certain things you can do, certain methods that have proven themselves throughout the years. So here is my final list, given in no particular order, of thoughts to help you see your potential as a successful worker with children.

1. List your resources.

You probably have more things going for you than you ever realized. Rather than looking at what you don't have and can't do, let's list the resources that we do accumulate over the years.

Knowledge

This book is a good start in the process for preparing for ministry; but by all means don't stop here. Check out every seminar that might provide the training you need. Read everything you can. There are many other good books that can help you. I have provided a list of favorites in the back of this book. Find friends who know things you don't. They are always a great source of help and can offer encouragement during hard times.

Experience

You cannot learn to swim by reading books. You need to get into the water. The more you work with children the better you will become at doing the things that really work. After a while you will develop your own style and realize that you have some great experiences under your belt that will be a help.

When a worker applies for a job his resumé tells what he has done before. Assumably, these experiences will help him in the future. Get all the experience you can. Volunteer to work with children, with parents, and with other workers. You will often finish a busy day having learned something about kids you never knew before. When Paul wrote young Timothy to "stir up the gift of God that is in you," I think I know what he meant (2 Tim. 1:6). I remember a swarm of bees in my grandmother's backyard. I was fascinated as I watched the insects seemingly frozen in midair. Then I had an idea. I found a large rock, measured my retreat, threw the rock as hard as I could and headed for the kitchen door. I stirred up something I will never forget!

I think Paul meant something like that. "Timothy, get busy doing everything you can. God has given you a gift. The more experience you get, the more you will refine your gift and the more effective you will become." Every day can make you better at the things you want to do to help boys and girls know and follow Christ.

Relationships

People are a most valuable resource. Many times I have called a friend to borrow a piece of equipment, to ask a question or to find a shoulder to cry on. Do what you can for others who are serving Christ. You don't do it for this reason, but you will find they will be there when you need their help.

Some of the most faithful workers I have ever recruited were people whose children I had helped in the past. Every time you do something to help someone you are building a treasury of relationships that will mean a lot in years to come. One of the greatest benefits of being a Christian (in my opinion, anyway) is the relationships within the body of Christ that help us live, succeed, and grow.

Money

You will never have enough of this, but some is available. God is not broke. He still owns those cattle on all of those hills. But He certainly isn't going to give it all to you (or to me, either.) We often think that a little more money would solve our problems, when it would seldom help that much.

The dollars we do have belong to the Lord. We must learn to use this resource with much care. Sometimes we become careless with our use of money. The Bible teaches us that God will entrust us with true spiritual riches based on our faithfulness in using of the money we have (Luke 16:11).

You may need to raise more money than your church can provide. I have found that God's people are quick to give to a project where the value is explained and apparent. Our children's choir often presented concerts at other churches, so we needed our own sound equipment to take along on the trips. I remember the day I realized we needed $1300 for a new sound control board, and we had no money at all. However, we did have a lot of parents who believed in what we were doing. I sent a note home that clearly explained our need. Eight days later the money was in hand. Almost every one of the one hundred families gave something, some only a dollar or two. Many gave five or ten dollars and several gave twenty-five or fifty dollars. One man had five hundred dollars to contribute. The need was there and God had the people to meet the need.

Never consider money a prohibiting obstacle. If your need is real and if your ministry is pure, God will take care of your needs. Sometimes the lack of funds is God's way of telling you not to buy. (That's why borrowing is so dangerous. God has no way to protect you from buying what you do not need.) But the Lord has always provided for the *needs* of ministries close to his heart.

Time

In one way we all have the same amount of this resource. In another way we do not. That is why Jesus warned us, "I must work the works of him that sent me, while it is day: the night cometh, when no man can work" (John 9:4). When you meet a child you do not know how long you have. She could move away or her parents could prevent her from involvement in your ministry.

Some kids were playing guns while waiting for the school bus. The sister took the toy gun from the playroom and "Bang!" her brother was dead. Not to be outdone, the "dead" brother went to the hall closet, took his father's shotgun, and "Bang!" his sister was dead. But the gun was loaded and the girl was with the Lord before the ambulance had arrived.

That kind of thing doesn't happen often, but it stands to remind us that we must take advantage of the time we do have. When that little girl sat in Junior Church the week before, none of us knew what would happen. That was my last chance. Never again would I have the opportunity to present the Gospel, share God's love or teach the Word of God to this precious child.

We can so easily waste time in Sunday School. The class I told you about in a previous chapter wasted almost the entire class period with registration and other nonessential activities. If we forget why we are there, we talk about other things and we waste another hour.

Your teaching should follow the total teaching philosophy that states:

Everything I do in class is for the purpose of helping me accomplish my lesson aims

Let's think along other lines. What time does your Sunday School (or the program where you serve) begin? Maybe 9:30? 9:45? 10:00? None of these is the correct answer. Your program begins when the first child arrives! If you are still setting up, looking for supplies and getting yourself organized as the children arrive, your lack of planning could have undesired results.

- You will waste precious time that could be used to teach the early-comers.

- Your children will become bored because there is nothing to do.

- The absence of planned activities could lead to discipline problems.

William Penn warned that time is "what we want most, but...what we use worst." When we run out of money we can always get more. But we can never get more time; our supply is limited in the strictest sense of the word. Opportunities come and go. Our time is short. It is a resource we must wisely use.

Facilities

You need to consider your existing facilities – the buildings and grounds that are available for regular use – from a new perspective. What space can you use that is being wasted now? Can you move this class here and that class there so everyone will have what they need and space is not wasted?

But what about other facilities? Are there camps (look in the phone book), parks or other facilities available that you can rent or borrow? Does a member have a farm with a big empty barn for that Western Round-Up? Do you have a friend with a pool big enough for parties and activities? Have you found a man with a boat yet? Make your own list of facilities that you might need in the future. Think through what you already have. You may have more there than you realize.

Equipment and supplies

Take care of equipment that you have purchased at great expense as well as the little things that can be lost unless you are careful. Always have extra projector bulbs on hand. Mark all of your equipment so it will be less likely to "walk away."

Make an inventory of the pencils, tape, craft supplies, paint, and other supplies you need on a regular basis or might need in the future. Will a print shop save you scraps of paper cut from printing jobs? Does a member have a business that can supply you with needed items for crafts and teaching projects?

Perhaps you use other kinds of supplies in your ministry. Learn to accumulate without being a pack rat. Learn to keep on hand the things you might need regularly. Make a file of catalogs where you can find supplies you need less often.

Influence

As you earn the respect of the children, their parents, the church leaders and the people in the community, you will find that your influence is one of your most valuable resources. A little push every now and then will encourage the people you really need to help you, involve kids in your program, and get stalled projects moving again.

The blessing and power of God

This is the one resource you cannot afford to ignore. Without the touch of heaven our efforts are in vain. The best organization cannot replace the work of the Holy Spirit of God in our ministry. Nothing eternal can be done in our own effort. God does not need us. He has lovingly chosen to use us in His work. So often our activity for Him is really for our own good. We enjoy it, like being busy with nice people, and need to feel we are doing something worthwhile. We are not just doing nice things to help out others. We are involved in the work of Almighty God. We cannot do that by ourselves.

Our resources are many. Properly considered and prayerfully used, these resources can provide what we need to get the job done.

2.   Meet the basic needs of children.

Remember something we learned together in an earlier chapter?

All good salesmen understand this important principle: If you want to make a sale you must look for a need the buyer has that you can meet, even if the buyer does not realize the need exists!

All children have needs that are often more felt than understood. They cannot explain these needs, but know something is wrong if their needs are not met. Here, in my opinion, are four of the most important needs children have.

Love and security

Like adults, children are afraid of the unknown. They need to know everything is all right, that they are safe and they are loved. It is the job of the children's worker to be certain the kids feel secure. Be especially sensitive to visitors and to children who just moved from out of town. A child who is causing discipline problems is often a child who needs to know that everything is okay. Maybe there is a problem at home. Perhaps there is fear that another child will hurt or laugh or do something that is more than the child can bear. Remember that they are children and must be treated with sensitive, gentle words and actions.

Acceptance

Children need to feel they are part of the group. Every class has social outcasts that need your help. Be quick to get visitors involved in non-threatening ways. Do not let groups of friends turn into cliques that leave out others. Make every child feel he or she is important and is a part of the group. Work to make every child feel he or she is your favorite.

One neat secret is to give awards for everything, especially Christian character. Be sure every child succeeds at something for which he or she can be recognized.

Realize it is your job to listen to your kids. You may hear the same jokes every year. You will know when to laugh after the third time!

Never get angry with a child. There is a boundary which, if crossed, will take you past your opportunity to help that boy or girl. Stay as far away from it as you can.

New experiences

Children bore quickly and need new experiences to keep them interested. You can easily get in a rut in your Bible teaching. It is such a shame to bore kids with the Word of God when we have before us the most exciting ideas and truths in the world.

Plan activities that will meet your children's needs for thrill and adventure. Again vary your teaching methods. Give it your best.

Meeting needs takes the presence of caring people. That amazing truth should overflow from our churches. Love is the tie that binds us together and causes us to love the world.

Has a visitor ever come to your class who did not return? There was, most likely, a reason. Either you did not do what the visitor wanted you to do or you did something he really did not like. A wise teacher will be sensitive to what is going on in the lives of children.

George Gallup, Jr., has provided us his own list of the six basic needs of young people. These thoughts provide another perspective on successful ministry to children.[2]

1. The need to believe that life is meaningful and has a purpose.
2. The need for a sense of community and deeper relationships.
3. The need to be appreciated and loved.
4. The need to be listened to and heard.
5. The need to feel that one is growing in faith.
6. The need for practical help in developing a mature faith.

You have read a lot about meeting needs in this book. Our job is to discover and to meet them.

3. Reach children through their strengths in order to strengthen their weaknesses.

Every child is good at something. I told you I was a shy child, not very good at sports. But I discovered that I was good at music. This interest is what provided my chance to be somebody special.

Never let a child fail. Begin at what he can do and use his strengths to reach into his life.

4. Be flexible in your methods, inflexible in your convictions.

Some things that work now will not work in ten years. People who believe in the infallibility and authority of Scripture (as I hope you do) are prone to a common error. We equate our methods with scriptural truth and strongly hold to both. We would have made good Pharisees.

Are the piano and organ the only instruments suitable for church? The stringed instruments with which we are to praise God (Ps. 150:4) were closer to guitars.

Must Sunday School come between breakfast and the morning worship service? Some churches have found better success on Sunday afternoon. A few find another day better for small group Bible study, limiting Sundays to group worship.

How about drama? And taped background tracks for soloists? Some churches think God only wants us to use a Steinway or a Baldwin when playing His music. And I could list lots of other things that some folks are sure were invented in heaven. But they are wrong. So adapt to the times. Filmstrip projectors have given way to VCRs. Music that speaks to the singers and the hearers is commonly used. Do what works, but never change your convictions.

What follows is my editorial opinion. If music communicates a message (even without lyrics), then music alone can also communicate a wrong message. We certainly want to use music that relates to the kids. But some things happening in the world today are wrong and we need to know what they are. Perhaps much is happening (not only in music but in other areas as well) that hinders our ultimate objective: to help children become more like Christ. Somewhere between the legalistic right and the permissive left lies an area of ministry where Christ is honored.

Read your Bible. Decide what you feel about right and wrong. Ask yourself how God feels about it. Make your decisions firm, never compromising your convictions. Never confuse your personal preferences with Scriptural principles. That may be the hardest part of all.

5.   Never underestimate the importance of what you do.

You cannot judge the success or failure of your ministry by the response of the parents. Moms and dads forget to say, "Thanks." Do not take it personally. They sometimes concentrate on what you did not do, forgetting all you did. Ignore that. Do not be easily offended. We are really doing this work for Christ, and He will reward us well.

Nothing we do for children is ever lost. They may grow and forget about many of the things we do, but our ministry becomes a part of their hearts for the rest of their lives. Today I met a 32-year-old who had once been a sixth-grader in a Junior Church I directed twenty years ago. Even though she memorized her Bible verse each week, she had never been called on to recite her assignment. Each child was given a number on a handwritten ticket that matched the number in a big bowl. I would choose a number and the chosen child would then come forward to recite the verse before the one hundred other children.

The day finally came when Gloria could stand it no longer. She prayed all week, asking the Lord that I might choose her. She promised that if she won she would never spend the two dollars that was to be given away as the prize that special week. On the big morning that followed her week of prayer I chose a ticket that matched the "33" on the little card she had been given. Proudly, she came forward, recited the verse, and won the money. And twenty years later, she showed me those two dollar bills and that little ticket stub she still carries in her purse. That was a big day for her that she will never forget. We have no idea how much influence we have on those little faces in front of us.

Children hear more than we think they hear. They think we hung the moon. We are their heroes. The little things we do are big in the eyes of the children. The promises we fail to keep can break their hearts.

We look for results, forgetting that effective ministry takes time. We are laying one brick at a time, all part of a majestic structure that will become a human life.

So there is the need, these are the methods, here are the tools. We are the missing piece of the puzzle, the most important part of all. Why God entrusted this work to us I do not know; but I am glad He did. It is our chance to build something that will last forever.

---

[2]Quoted in *Group Magazine*, "6 Basic Needs of Young People" (page 16; June-August 1992) © Group Publishing. Adapted from *The Religious Life of Young Americans* (pp. 12-14) by George H. Gallup, Jr. and Robert Bezilla. © 1992 by The George H. Gallup International Institute.

Chapter Eight

REVIEW QUESTIONS:

1. What are nine resources we accumulate that will help us in ministry?

2. What is the "total teaching" philosophy?

3. What are the basic needs of children?

DISCUSSION QUESTIONS:

1. How would you evaluate your present resources that are available to help you minister to children?

2. What can you do to help children feel a sense of community and build deep relationships?

3. What are your basic convictions that will guide your ministry to children? How will your convictions affect the things you do?

BIBLIOGRAPHY

Anderson, R.S. *Christians Who Counsel.* Grand Rapids, MI: Zondervan Publishing House, 1990.

Anthony, Michael J. and the Christian Education faculty of Biola University–Talbot School of Theology. *Foundations of Ministry: An Introduction to Christian Education for a New Generation.* Wheaton, IL: Victor Books, 1992.

Ball, A. and B. *Basic Camp Management.* Martinsville, IN: American Camping Association, 1987.

Barnes, Robert G., Jr. *Raising Confident Kids.* Grand Rapids, MI: Zondervan Publishing House, 1992.

Barrett, Ethel. *Storytelling—It's Easy!* Grand Rapids, MI: Zondervan Publishing House, 1960.

Beechick, R. *Teaching Juniors: Both Heart and Head.* Denver, CO: Accent Books, 1981.

—. *Teaching Primaries: Understanding How They Think and How They Learn.* Denver, CO: Accent Books, 1985.

Berk, Laura E. *Child Development,* 2nd ed. Needham Heights, MA: Allyn & Bacon, 1990.

Blankenbaker, Frances. *What the Bible Is All About for Young Explorers.* Ventura, CA: Regal Books, 1986.

—. ed. *Teacher Training Manual.* Ventura, CA: International Center for Learning, 1982.

Bolton, Barbara. *How to Do Bible Learning Activities for Grades 1-6.* Ventura, CA: Gospel Light Publications, 1982.

Bolton, Barbara and Charles T. Smith. *Everything You Want to Know About Teaching Children, Grades 1-6.* Ventura, CA: Regal Books, 1987.

Brawner, Jim. *Connections: Using Personality Types to Draw Parents and Kids Closer.* Chicago, IL: Moody Press, 1991.

Brown, Marion E., and Marjorie G. Prentice. *Christian Education in the Year 2000.* Valley Forge, PA: Judson Press, 1984.

Brown, Lowell. E. *Sunday School Standards.* Revised edition. Ventura, CA: International Center for Learning, 1986.

Burton, T. *The Trainable Mentally Retarded.* Columbus, OH: Merrill Publishing, Co., 1975.

Bustanoby, Andy. *Single Parenting.* Grand Rapids, MI: Zondervan Publishing House, 1992.

Campbell, Ross. *How to Really Love Your Child.* Wheaton, IL: Victor Books, 1977.

Campbell, Ross. *Kids Who Follow, Kids Who Don't.* Wheaton, IL: Victor Books, 1977.

Carter, Wm. Lee. *Kid Think.* Dallas, TX: Word Publishing, 1991.

Chall, Sally Lehman. *Making God Real to Your Children.* Old Tappan, NJ: Fleming H. Revell, 1991.

Chamberlain, Eugene. *When Can a Child Believe.* Nashville, TN: Broadman Press, 1973.

Chapin, Alice. *Building Your Child's Faith.* Nashville, TN: Thomas Nelson Publishers, 1990.

Cherne, Jacquelyn. *The Learning Disabled in Your Church School.* St. Louis, MO: Concordia, 1983.

Cionca, John R. *The Troubleshooting Guide to Christian Education.* Denver, CO: Accent Publications, 1986.

Claerbaut, David. *Urban Ministry.* Grand Rapids, MI: Zondervan Publishing House, 1983.

Clark, Robert E., Lin Johnson and Allyn K. Sloat. *Christian Education: Foundation for the Future*. Chicago, IL: Moody Press, 1991.

Clark, Robert E., J. Brubaker and Roy B. Zuck. *Childhood Education in the Church*. Chicago, IL: Moody Press, 1986.

Coleman, Lucien E., Jr. *How to Teach the Bible*. Nashville, TN: Broadman Press, 1980.

Colson, Howard P., and Raymond M. Rigdon. *Understanding Your Church's Curriculum*. Revised edition. Nashville, TN: Broadman Press, 1981.

Cooper, John A. *Working with Deaf Persons in Sunday School*. Nashville, TN: Convention Press, 1982.

Cuthbertson, Duane. *Raising Your Child, Not Your Voice*. Wheaton, IL: Victor Books, 1986.

Daniel, Eleanor. *The ABC's of VBS*. Cincinnati, OH: Standard Publishers, 1984.

Dargatz, Jan. 52 *Simple Ways to Build Your Child's Self-Esteem*. Nashville, TN: Thomas Nelson Publishers, 1991.

Delnay, Robert G. *Teach As He Taught*. Chicago, IL: Moody Press, 1987.

Dobson, James. *Hide or Seek*. Old Tappan, NJ: Fleming H. Revell, 1977.

Dobson, James. *The New Dare to Discipline*. Wheaton, IL: Tyndale House Publishers, Inc., 1992.

Drescher, John. *Seven Things Children Need*. Scottsdale, PA: Herald Press, 1988.

Dunn, Kenneth J. and Rita. *Teaching Students Through Their Individual Learning Styles: A Practical Approach*. Reston, VA: Prentice-Hall, 1978.

Edge, Findley B. *Teaching for Results*. Nashville, TN: Broadman Press, 1959.

Elkind, David. *The Hurried Child: Growing Up Too Fast Too Soon.* Reading, MA: Addison-Wesley Publishing Co., Inc., 1988.

—. *A Sympathetic Understanding of the Child, Birth to Sixteen.* Boston, MA: Allyn and Bacon, Inc., 1974.

Fine, E. and B.J. *Teachers Are Made, Not Born.* Cincinnati, OH: Standard Press, 1990.

Fortune, Dan and Katie. *Discover Your Children's Gifts.* Old Tappan, NJ: Fleming H. Revell, 1989.

Friedeman, M. *The Master Plan of Teaching.* Wheaton, IL: Victor Books, 1990.

Furnish, Dorothy Jean. *Experiencing the Bible with Children.* Nashville, TN: Abington Press, 1990.

Gaebelein, Frank E. *The Pattern of God's Truth.* Chicago, IL: Moody Press, 1968.

Gangel, Kenneth O. *Twenty-four Ways to Improve Your Teaching.* Wheaton, IL: Victor Books, 1986.

Gangel, Kenneth O., and Howard Hendricks, eds. *The Christian Educator's Handbook on Teaching.* Wheaton, IL: Victor Books, 1988.

Garborg, Rolf. *The Family Blessing.* Dallas, TX: Word Publishing, 1990.

Gibson, Joyce, and Eleanor Hance. *You Can Teach Juniors & Middlers.* Wheaton, IL: Victor Books, 1981.

Gilbert, Larry. *Team Ministry: A Guide to Spiritual Gifts and Lay Involvement.* Lynchburg, VA: Church Growth Institute, 1987.

Hadley, G. *How to Teach the Mentally Retarded.* Wheaton, IL: Victor Books, 1978.

Halbert, Barbara Lee. *Creative Discipline for Young Children.* Nashville, TN: Broadman Press, 1980.

Hancock, Maxine. *Creative, Confident Children.* Wheaton, IL: Harold Shaw Publishers, 1992.

Hart, Archibald D. *Children & Divorce.* Dallas, TX: Word Publishing, 1989.

Haystead, Wes. *The 3,000-Year-Old Guide to Parenting: Wisdom from Proverbs for Today's Parents.* Ventura, CA: Regal Books, 1992.

Hendricks, Howard G. *Teaching to Change Lives.* Portland, OR: Multnomah Press, 1987.

Hesselgrave, David J. *Communicating Christ Cross-Culturally.* 2nd edition. Grand Rapids, MI: Zondervan Publishing House, 1991.

Heusser, D-B and Phyllis. *Children as Partners in the Church.* Valley Forge, PA: Judson Press, 1985.

International Children's Bible: New Century Version. Dallas, TX: Word Publishing, 1988.

Ingle, Clifford, ed. *Children and Conversion.* Nashville, TN: Broadman Press, 1970.

Johnson, D.W. *The Care and Feeding of Volunteers.* Nashville, TN: Abingdon Press, 1978.

Kessler, Jay. *Raising Responsible Kids.* Brentwood, Tennessee: Wolgemuth & Hyatt, Publishers, Inc, 1991.

Kessler, Jay; Beers, Ron; and Neff, LaVonne, editors. *Parents & Children.* Wheaton, IL: Victor Books, 1986.

Kincaid, Jorie. *The Power of Modeling.* Colorado Springs, CO: NavPress, 1989

Lawson, Michael S. and Robert J. Choun, Jr. *Directing Christian Education: The Changing Role of the Christian Education Specialist.* Chicago, IL: Moody Press, 1992.

LeBar, Lois E., edited by James E. Plueddeman. *Education That Is Christian*. Wheaton, IL: Victor Books, 1989.

Lehman, Kevin. *The Birth Order Book*. Old Tappan, NJ: Fleming H. Revell, 1985.

Lester, Andrew D. *When Children Suffer*. Philadelphia: The Westminster Press, 1987.

Lewis, Paul. *40 Ways to Teach Your Child Values*. Wheaton, IL: Tyndale House Publishers, Inc., 1985.

Leypoldt, Martha. *Learning is Change*. Valley Forge, PA: Judson Press, 1971.

Lingenfelter, Sherwood G., and Marvin K. Mayers. *Ministering Cross-Culturally*. Grand Rapids, MI: Baker Book House, 1986.

McDaniel, Elsiebeth. *You Can Teach Primaries*. Wheaton, IL: Victor Books, 1981.

McDowell, Josh and Dick Day. *How to Be a Hero to Your Kids*. Dallas, TX: Word Publishers, 1991.

McGinn, Linda R. *The Bible Answers Questions Children Ask*. Nashville, TN: Broadman Press, 1992.

Meier, Paul D. *Christian Child-Rearing and Personality Development*. Grand Rapids, MI: Baker Book House, 1977.

Milburn, Joyce. *Helping Your Children Love Each Other*. Minneapolis, MN: Bethany House Publishers, 1983.

Minear, Ralph and Proctor, William. *Kids Who Have Too Much*. Nashville, TN: Thomas Nelson Publishers, 1989.

Murray, Andrew. *How to Raise Your Children for Christ*. Minneapolis, MN: Bethany House Publishers, 1975.

Narramore, Bruce. *Your Child's Hidden Needs.* Old Tappan, NJ: Fleming H. Revell, 1990.

Ng, David and Thomas, Virginia. *Children in the Worshipping Community.* Atlanta, GA: John Knox Press, 1981.

Owen, Herb. *Junior Ministries Manual.* Lynchburg, VA: Acorn Children's Publications, 1987.

——. producer. *The Complete Kids Choir Video Guide.* Videotape. Brentwood, TN: Brentwood Music Co., 1991.

Pazmiño, Robert E. *Foundational Issues in Christian Education.* Grand Rapids, MI: Baker Book House, 1988.

Perkins, Bill with Cooper, Rod. *Kids in Sports.* Portland, OR: Multnomah Press, 1989.

Pierson, Jim, and Bob Korth, eds. *Reaching Out to Special People: A Resource for Ministry with Persons Who Have Disabilities.* Cincinnati, OH: Standard Publications, 1989.

Price, Max B. *Understanding Today's Children.* Nashville, TN: Convention Press, 1982.

Raus, Bob. *Ministry Through Camping.* Nashville, TN: Convention Press, 1990.

Reimer, Kathie, *1001 Ways to Introduce Your Child to God.* Wheaton, IL: Tyndale House Publishers, Inc., 1992.

Richards, Lawrence O. *Christian Education: Seeking to Become Like Jesus Christ.* Grand Rapids, MI: Zondervan Publishing House, 1975.

——. *Children: The Lively Learners.* Elgin, IL: David C. Cook, 1988.

——. *Children's Ministry: Nurturing Faith Within the Family of God.* Grand Rapids, MI: Zondervan Publishing House, 1983.

—. *Creative Bible Teaching.* Chicago, IL: Moody Press, 1970.

—. *International Children's Bible Handbook.* Dallas, TX: Word Publishing, 1989.

—. *Teachers: Teaching with Love.* Elgin, IL: David C. Cook, 1988.

Roehlkepartain, Jolele L., ed. *Children's Ministry That Works: The Basics & Beyond.* Loveland, CO: Group Books, 1991.

Schaefer, Charles E. *How to Talk to Children About Really Important Things.* New York, NY: Harper & Row, Publishers, Inc., 1989.

Schock, Bernie. *Parents, Kids & Sports.* Chicago, IL: Moody Press, 1987.

Schorr, Vernie. *Recruiting, Training, and Developing Volunteer Children's Workers.* Cincinatti, OH: Standard Publishing, 1991.

Sears, William, M.D. *Christian Parenting and Child Care.* Nashville, TN: Thomas Nelson Publishers, 1991.

Senter III, Mark. *Recruiting Volunteers in the Church.* Wheaton, IL: Victor Books, 1983.

Shelly, Judith Allen. *The Spiritual Needs of Children.* Downers Grove, IL: InterVaristy Press, 1982.

Smalley, Gary. *The Key to Your Child's Heart.* Dallas, TX: Word Publishing, 1992.

Smalley, Gary and John Trent. *The Blessing.* New York, NY: Picket Books, 1990.

Smith, Daniel H. *How to Lead a Child to Christ.* Chicago, IL: Moody Press, 1987.

Steinbron, Melvin J. *Can the Pastor Do It Alone?* Ventura, CA: Regal Books, 1987.

Stevens, R. Paul. *Liberating the Laity: Equipping All the Saints for Ministry.* Downers Grove, IL: InterVaristy Press, 1985.

Tidwell, Charles A. *Educational Ministry of a Church.* Nashville, TN: Broadman Press, 1982.

Trumbull, H. Clay. *Hints on Child Training.* Brentwood, TN: Wolgemuth & Hyatt, Publishers, Inc., 1989.

Tucker, Drew. *Coaching Basketball: A Complete Guide for the Recreational Coach.* Nashville, TN: Convention Press, 1991.

Understanding Sunday School. Wheaton, IL: Evangelical Training Association, 1981.

Urban, Hal. *20 Things I Want My Kids to Know.* Nashville, TN: Thomas Nelson Publishers, 1992.

Westerhoff, John. *Will Our Children Have Faith?* New York, NY: Seabury Press, 1976.

Westing, H.J. *Evaluate and Grow.* Wheaton, IL: Victor Books, 1984.

White, Joe. *The Gift of Self-Esteem.* Sisters, OR: Questar Publishers, 1989.

Wilhoit, Jim, and Leland Ryken. *Effective Bible Teaching.* Grand Rapids, MI: Baker Book House, 1988.

Wilkinson, Bruce and Boa, Kenneth. *Talk Thru the Bible.* Nashville, TN: Thomas Nelson Publishers, 1983.

Willis, W.R. *Developing the Teacher in You.* Wheaton, IL: Victor Books, 1990.

—. *Make Your Teaching Count.* Wheaton, IL: Victor Books, 1985.

Willmington, H.L. *Willmington's Guide to the Bible.* Wheaton, IL: Tyndale House Publishers, Inc., 1981.

Wilson, Ken. *The Obedient Child.* Ann Arbor, MI: Servant Books, 1988.

Wolterstorff, Nicholas. *Education for Responsible Action.* Grand Rapids, MI: William B. Eerdmans Publishing Co., 1980.

Wooden, Kenneth. *Teaching Children to Pray.* Grand Rapids, MI: Zondervan Publishing House, 1992.

Wortley, Judy. *The Recruiting Remedy.* Elgin, IL: David C. Cook, 1990.

Wright, H. Norman. *Help, I'm a Camp Counselor.* Ventura, CA: Regal Books, 1986.

—. *The Power of a Parent's Words.* Ventura, CA: Regal Books, 1991.

Zuck, Roy B. *The Holy Spirit in Your Teaching.* Revised and expanded. Wheaton, IL: Victor Books, 1984.

Zuck, Roy B. and Robert E. Clark, eds. *Childhood Education and the Church.* Chicago, IL: Moody Press, 1975.

Publishers of Curriculum, Children's Programs, Teaching Resources, and Teacher Training Materials

Accent Publications, 12110 W. Sixth Avenue, Box 15337, Denver, CO 80215, (800) 525-5550, (303) 988-5300.

Acorn Children's Publications, Liberty University, Lynchburg, VA 24506, (804) 582-2000.

Awana Clubs International, One East Bode Road, Streamwood, IL 60107, (708) 213-2000.

Child Evangelism Fellowship, Inc., Warrenton, MO 63383, (314) 456-4321.

Christian Service Brigade, P.O. Box 150, Wheaton, IL 60189, (708) 665-0630.

David. C. Cook Publishing, 850 N. Grove Ave., Elgin, IL 60120, (800) 323-7543.

Gospel Light Publications, Box 6309, Oxnard, CA 93031, (800) 446-7735.

Group Publications, Box 481, Loveland, CO 80539, (303) 669-3836.

Pioneer Clubs, P.O. Box 788, Wheaton, IL 60189, (708) 293-1600.

Scripture Press Publications, 1825 College Avenue, Wheaton, IL 60187, (800) 323-9409.

Standard Publishing, 8121 Hamilton Avenue, Cincinnati, OH 45231, (800) 543-1301.

Word of Life Fellowship, Inc. (Word of Life Clubs), P.O. Box 600, Schroon Lake, NY 12870, (518) 532-7111.

Scriptures Relating to Our Ministry to Children

"Give ear, O my people, to my law: incline your ears to the words of my mouth. I will open my mouth in a parable: I will utter dark sayings of old: Which we have heard and known, and our fathers have told us. We will not hide them from their children, showing to the generation to come the praises of the Lord, and his strength, and his wonderful works that he hath done. For he established a testimony in Jacob, and appointed a law in Israel, which he commanded our fathers, that they should make them known to their children: That the generation to come might know them, even the children which should be born; who should arise and declare them to their children: That they might set their hope in God, and not forget the words of God, but keep his commandments: And might not be as their fathers, a stubborn and rebellious generation; a generation that set not their heart aright, and whose spirit was not stedfast with God." *Psalm 78:1-8*

"And these words, which I command thee this day, shall be in thine heart: And thou shalt teach them diligently unto thy children, and shalt talk of them when thou sittest in thine house, and when thou walkest by the way, and when thou liest down, and when thou risest up." *Deuteronomy 6:6-7*

"And the child grew, and waxed strong in spirit, and was in the deserts till the day of his showing unto Israel." *Luke 1:80*

"And Jesus increased in wisdom and stature, and in favour with God and man." *Luke 2:52*

"And he goeth up into a mountain, and calleth unto him whom he would: and they came unto him. And he ordained twelve, that they should be with him." *Mark 3:13, 14a*

"A student is not better than the teacher, but the student who has been fully trained will be like the teacher." *Luke 6:40 NCV*

"Jesus used stories to tell all these things to the people; he always used stories to teach them." *Matthew 13:34 NCV*

"So they read in the book of the law of God distinctly, and gave the sense, and caused them to understand the reading." *Nehemiah 8:8*

Launching a faith-building, life-changing children's ministry...

Most Christians are familiar with the age-old wisdom of Proverbs 22:6: *Train up a child in the way he should go. And when he is old he will not depart from it.* Although much of this responsiblity falls on the home, the church also has a role in training children, by giving biblical instruction and making the Bible come alive to them. The challenge is to provide a ministry that attracts and excites children so they will want to come and be a part of the church and will be drawn to Christ.

Providing an effective, *real* ministry that meets children's needs is crucial to their future - and the church's future. This packet was created to help you develop such a ministry.

The Complete Guide to Starting or Evaluating a Children's Ministry gives a strategy, a specific plan of action with a checklist to guide you and timetables to suggest when you might accomplish each step. Session guides for training workers and special material for the Pastor or Children's Pastor are included along with audiotapes containing instructions and lessons from the author.

To Order: Sign, Clip, and Mail Order Form Below or call 1-800-553-GROW

✂